Your
Wedding
A Planning Guide

Greg Friedman, O.F.M.

St.
Anthony
Messenger
Press

CINCINNATI, OHIO

Nihil Obstat: Rev. Thomas Richstatter, O.F.M.
          Rev. Robert L. Hagedorn

Imprimi Potést: Rev. John Bok, O.F.M.
          Provincial

Imprimatur: +James H. Garland, V.G.
          Archdiocese of Cincinnati
          February 22, 1991

The *nihil obstat* and *imprimatur* are a declaration that a book is considered to be free from doctrinal or moral error. It is not implied that those who have granted the *nihil obstat* and *imprimatur* agree with the contents, opinions or statements expressed.

Cover and book design by Julie Lonneman

ISBN 0-86716-117-5

©1991, Greg Friedman, O.F.M.
All rights reserved.

Published by St. Anthony Messenger Press
Printed in the U.S.A.

For Bob and Elaine

Acknowledgments

A number of years ago, St. Anthony Messenger Press published *Your Wedding*. It was written by Father Jeremy Harrington, a special person in my life: a wise teacher, a patient editor, a caring religious superior and a friend.

The years that have passed make this an appropriate time to update the material in *Your Wedding*. Because Father Jeremy's work in recent years has involved the important responsibility of caring for his Franciscan brothers in St. John the Baptist Province, as provincial minister, he could not undertake the task of revising *Your Wedding*. I am honored that St. Anthony Messenger Press asked me to try.

Rather than a simple revision, however, I have narrowed Jeremy's original focus in that book and written a new treatment. His original material formed the foundation for my approach, and some of his choice phrases have been "fraternally borrowed" and incorporated into my manuscript. I am grateful to Jeremy for his encouragement to me as a writer over the years, first as a magazine staff member under his editorship and then as a member of his provincial office staff.

I wish also to thank the couples who have allowed me to celebrate their wedding with them and the married couples who have permitted me to collaborate with them in marriage preparation ministry. Generous married and engaged couples and clergy also reviewed this text and offered criticisms and suggestions.

When I was a boy, my brother Mark and I used to put on puppet shows together, choosing songs and designing elaborate productions. As adults, we work together on "productions" of a different sort. He is a church musician, gives concerts and plays weddings and has worked with hundreds of engaged couples.

From time to time Mark and I collaborate in the liturgical setting and recapture some of the creativity and fun we had playing together as children. When it comes to wedding planning, I naturally turn to him as my "personal expert" on music.

He has discussed with me on more than one occasion the principles he uses in assembling musical programs for weddings. As I was writing this book we sat down and distilled his principles into "ten tips" for Chapter Six. Under each "tip" I have paraphrased Mark's reflections as he has shared them with me over the years. In reading them, you are not only sharing the expertise of one liturgical musician, but also the questions and concerns of the many couples he has assisted.

I am indebted to my Franciscan colleagues, Fathers Jerry Kaelin and Tom Richstatter, and to *The Order of the Mass: Guidelines*, by Eugene A. Walsh, S.S., for the ideas on the "flow" of wedding liturgy which I have used in my Introduction.

Finally, my dedication is to two good friends who have shared the witness of their sacrament of marriage in friendship with me.

Contents

Contents

Introduction
Getting Started With Your Wedding Plans

Years ago, after a home Mass, I asked the people gathered around the card-table altar in the living room to write down their reactions to the liturgy. One youngster wrote a response I have kept to this day: "As a kid, this was the best Mass I've ever been to. P.S. I've been to a lot of Masses."

Well, I've been to a lot of weddings, and I'd like yours to be as good a celebration as you can make it. I hope it truly expresses all you believe about yourselves, your relationship and your God—who *is* interested in what you promise together. That's what this book is about. I want to help you make good choices as you plan your wedding so it will be the best it can be.

This book is not a *marriage* preparation guide. Many fine resources are available to help you identify the crucial issues facing you as a couple in the rest of your lives together. Neither is it a complete guide to planning a wedding—invitations, reception and all. Rather, my purpose is to help you focus on your wedding *liturgy*. To do that, I will briefly explore not only the *what* and *how* of the celebration, but also the *who* (you who celebrate the sacrament of marriage) and the *why* (the reasons for the religious setting).

Getting in Touch With a Parish

We often see the Church as an institution that is the same everywhere. But anyone who has attended more than one wedding knows that, although all weddings are about two people becoming one, ceremonies and

1

externals can be very different from place to place. In the same way, Church exists in many different expressions known by the names *diocese* and *parish*, and does things in different ways in different locales.

What you read here has been carefully chosen so as not to conflict with either general norms or local practice. Still, you may encounter specific procedures where you will have your wedding, specifics that can't be completely covered in a book such as this.

How do you find out what those specifics are? Begin where the local Church begins—at a parish. It is customary (and Church law) to celebrate a wedding in the home parish of either the bride or the groom. The custom arose from the fact that we more easily identify with a community where we live. But not all of us can conveniently celebrate in such a place, for a variety of reasons. Often couples schedule their wedding in their parents' parish, in a college chapel or in a setting that meets other needs (a comfortable place to worship, a place convenient for guests traveling from out of town, and so on). Church regulations recognize such needs, and exceptions can be made in many cases.

Another local specific concerns how far in advance to contact a parish for a wedding. The Church wants you to have plenty of time to do the best possible planning.

Each parish also has its own needs and guidelines. These may affect such items as scheduling (for example, registered parishioners ordinarily get priority), church decorations, inviting another priest or deacon to have your wedding and even the kind of music and other specifics you can choose. Please approach your situation with patience and openness. There are probably valid reasons for a parish to ask certain things of you as you plan your wedding.

If you've been given this book by the priest or deacon helping you plan your wedding, you've already taken the first step. If you've picked it up from a book rack or bookstore, you may need to know how to start.

The parish bulletin of the Church where you worship

on Sundays will normally contain guidelines for wedding arrangements. It is best to *call* the parish office to set up an appointment. If you are not a regular parishioner anywhere, the parish nearest where you live is the place to begin. Your diocesan Family Life Office also can help you get started.

When you call a parish, explain that you are planning to get married. The person who answers the phone will usually explain what you need to do—especially putting you in touch with a priest or deacon who will work with you. In some parishes, a married couple may be assigned to the same role.

In addition to the parish priest, deacon or "marriage ministry" couple, another good resource person is the church musician. He or she is familiar with parish regulations about music and other liturgical details, can explain some of the reasons behind the guidelines and help you head off problems.

Before You Do Any Planning...

You've probably made some essential wedding planning decisions. (I suspect some brides have chosen their bridesmaids even before getting an engagement ring!) But in order for your wedding to be a rich, faith-filled experience, it might help to step back and look at your wedding ceremony as a whole first. Going slow on some of the details and giving time to the bigger picture will help you better organize and choose among those many details.

So hold off counting the bridesmaids before you read on. Here are five "big picture" considerations:

1) *Make your wedding prayerful.* Your marriage is celebrated in a church setting because we believe it is a sacrament, a sign that expresses the reality: You are one in the Lord. (More on this in Chapter Two.)

That's heavy theology! At this point in planning, you may be more interested in where the bridesmaids will stand in the church sanctuary—a valid concern. But the

3

reason you're in church to begin with is to touch base with what God is doing for and with you.

Prayer puts you in touch with God as a "silent partner" in your relationship. Your wedding will be prayerful if you begin to pray together now, as a couple—as you meet with your priest or deacon, at other times during your engagement and at the rehearsal. You can set a pattern now for your whole marriage.

2) *Plan well.* Planning takes time. Pray and reflect on the kind of ceremony you would like to have. Consider all the elements, not just the dresses, tuxedos and flowers. Pray over the Scripture readings. Look at resource materials for ideas and suggestions. Talk to friends who have recently been married and priests or deacons whose style of presiding you respect.

Good liturgy doesn't just happen. It takes planning.

3) *Know what you want—and why.* One pastor-friend of mine refused to let people toss rice after a wedding (guess who had to clean it up!) unless the couple could explain the custom. Not many knew it is an old symbol of fertility.

Another wedding custom calls for the father to escort his daughter down the aisle. You probably know that this practice comes from a past when the bride's permission to marry and financial matters were male-controlled. Though you might choose to follow the custom for sentimental reasons, I encourage you to question it—if only to involve the three other parents left in the pew to watch while Dad "gives away" his daughter.

It's a risk to challenge customs protecting this important moment of transition in your lives. But you can also create new ways to proclaim boldly what you are about in your wedding.

4) *Make your wedding personal.* Personalizing makes a wedding special. For many Catholics, it's one of the few times they get to plan a Church service uniquely their own.

So make it truly *your* wedding—not a clone of the last three you attended. Add personal touches to make the ceremony truly an expression of who you both are. (More on this later, too.)

One caution: be sure that any personal elements you include—a favorite poem or song, for example—are also general enough to be understood by those in attendance. What is special and meaningful to you as a couple may be baffling to your guests.

5) *Be consistent in planning.* In any liturgy, there ought to be consistency, a sense that the parts work together. The best way to ensure this is to have a *theme*, a statement which expresses what you are about.

You may or may not *state* the theme at the wedding itself—that's not essential. What's more important is to arrange things with a sense of proportion. For example, many couples include a candle ceremony in their wedding. Fine—but if it's just "another thing to do" without really expressing what you both are saying about your relationship and commitment, why include it?

A Special Consideration: Interfaith Marriage

Before we go look at wedding planning in more detail, we need to attend to an important consideration that will apply to some of you reading this book: those who come from two different faith traditions.

To begin with, your priest or deacon will help with the needed permissions and with the options you may pursue, thanks to the improved ecumenical climate of the post-Vatican II Church. For example, a Protestant minister may take part, doing readings, preaching, offering prayers drawn from his or her tradition. A joint meeting with all concerned may be useful before you get too far along in the planning.

Remember as you plan that religion is very personal, and so is the setting in which we practice it. Differences in practice can give rise to discomfort. For some people, simply entering the church of another denomination may be an awkward experience. Catholic practice limits the reception of Communion to Catholics only; at a wedding

5

this rule can exclude half of the congregation from participating.

You have the option of celebrating your wedding without a Mass. (If one party is not baptized, this is mandatory). If you are bringing together two different faith backgrounds, you should seriously consider this option.

A reminder for the *Catholic* party in the interfaith setting: You may need to explain gently to your parents or other family members why you've chosen *not* to have a Mass. This is a "teachable moment," one of many you will probably face as you start a life together that includes two different faith expressions.

This book assumes you will be in a Catholic parish setting—that alone may be a big step for some of your guests. Be sure that, as the ceremony begins, someone—the minister, priest or deacon—explains what is going to happen, when to sit and stand and so forth for those who may be new to the setting.

How This Book Can Help You Plan

The first three chapters of this book will explore three important issues that shed light on your liturgical planning: *who you are* as individuals and as a couple; *what your wedding means* in a "faith context"; and, finally, *why have it in a church setting* at all?

If you are interested in specifics (like music or when you actually say your vows), bear with me for a few pages. We'll get to those in Chapters Four through Eight. Then I will provide you with a special planning sheet to get organized.

Every chapter of the book has space for you to begin organizing your choices, first about the broader issues affecting your wedding liturgy and then about the more specific ones. It appears under the heading, "What Do You Want for Your Wedding?" You may want to have a pencil in hand as you read. (You may find it helpful to make a copy of the questions, answering them each

6

separately. Then share your answers with each other and perhaps with those who are assisting you in your wedding planning.)

Your wedding, as my friends from Catholic Engaged Encounter say, is only a day; your marriage is a *lifetime*. But getting off to a great start with your wedding liturgy will help provide a firm foundation.

Chapter One

Who Are You?

For a number of years, I was privileged to be a "team priest" for Catholic Engaged Encounter, a weekend program which seeks to help engaged couples prepare well for marriage. Each weekend, before getting into the expected issues of communication or sexuality, we always gave a talk entitled "Encounter With Me." I often wondered if it struck the engaged couples as odd to start a weekend about being together for life with an exclusive focus on self.

But the wise married couples who thought up Engaged Encounter had a good reason. You can't enter into a relationship without knowing *yourself* well. By now, well into the process of planning your married lives together, you probably are aware of your individual selves and your unique personalities, which, as you grow closer, are merging into a new reality: you as a couple.

Perhaps you've had some arguments, too, the result of the often uneven task of merging two lives. Different tastes, different ideas about money, different styles of decision-making—all can reflect the unique self which now finds itself evaluating everything in the light of another unique self. These arguments reveal different expectations and dreams—things you may need to sort out as you get to know each other better. (If you're like most of the engaged couples I know, this task is pretty exciting and full of energy. For some, even the arguments are fun!)

Knowing Yourself as a Person of Faith

As you plan your wedding liturgy, the wisdom of an "encounter with me" applies to how you are bringing together two unique selves in a moment of faith—and there is nothing so personal as the religious dimension of our lives.

I dislike partitioning some of life into the "religious" part—primarily because then we tend to wall that part off from the rest of our lives. (In the next chapter, I want to talk more about how our religion and our lives blend, especially in the moment of celebrating a wedding.) The fundamental choices you make about who you want to be and how you want to encounter God in your life are not simply "religious" choices. They are *human* choices, and they influence all of your life, including how you plan your wedding.

I'd like to invite you to take a moment to explore with yourself what you, as a person of faith, are bringing to your wedding day and—more importantly—to the married life that lies beyond.

No one is like me or you. Our uniqueness is apparent to those who know us well. Certainly the two of you as a couple can appreciate that. By now you share special secrets about each other which reveal your uniqueness to one another.

Who we are before God is very personal, even secret. Your image of God is like no one else's. How you pray is particular to you. And even though we belong to a community of faith, the Church, and share many beliefs and well-expressed statements of faith, we still have personal ways of talking about what we believe. Different cultures and different places have a variety of unique ways to celebrate our shared faith.

As you approach your wedding day and a public in-church proclamation of who you are before God—as individuals and as a couple—it may be tough to bring such personal thoughts and feelings to the surface. Getting in touch with them may be new to you. It may be even tougher to share those thoughts with your partner or with the people helping to prepare your wedding liturgy.

Part of the problem might be in making the leap from

10

what you can see and feel and experience about your own personal lives and the invisible, intangible dimension within you that has to do with your religious thoughts and feelings. And yet, you have a way to make such a leap (more like a *connection*)—in the very relationship you are about to celebrate.

From Human Love to God's Love

You would not be planning a wedding celebration were it not for love. Human love and friendship are among the deepest and greatest joys we can know. We seek them eagerly and hold fast to them. Friendship and love are also sure avenues into a life of faith. The feelings—both comfortable and uncomfortable—which we experience in human relationships can also accurately describe our relationship with God (which is another way to talk about *faith*).

A Franciscan friend of mine once said you can sum up the whole Bible as God saying "I love you" to the human family. That idea got me thinking: How many Bible stories are about one-to-one relationships between God and people? In the Old Testament, we read about Adam and Eve, Abraham and Sarah, Noah, Moses, Ruth, Judith and Esther, all having personal encounters with God— friendships with many of the same qualities as our human friendships. The New Testament is filled with similar stories.

The Bible stories seem to equate human and divine friendship. How I first meet a friend, the questions that arise in the friendship, the way we communicate, the signs that symbolize our relationship—all these and more happen when I come to know God as a friend, and, yes, as a lover. (The great mystics of our Christian tradition use passionate human love as a metaphor for the relationship between the human heart and the divine.)

Why not take some time now to reflect on what you have learned first as single persons and then as people in a couple relationship. What values move you? What signs have you chosen to mark your friendship? What doubts still afflict you? Then take that valuable learning a step further and allow it to teach you about the presence of God, as friend and lover, in your lives. What you discover will enliven the planning of the religious celebration of that love in your wedding liturgy.

What Do You Want for Your Wedding?

1) When you think about yourself as a person, what words do you use to describe yourself? (Name qualities, such as *patient, interesting, strong, gentle.*)

2) When you think about your partner as your *friend,* what words describe your relationship? (Again, what "quality" words come to mind?)

3) How do you think about God? What words do you use to describe God? (If it is difficult to get in touch with an image or idea of God, think back to an image from when you were younger.)

4) Finally, transfer the human qualities you explored in the first two questions to your current relationship with God. Try to share this with your partner. (It may help to begin with the difficulties or the changes you've experienced.)

Chapter Two
A Sacrament Is a Sign

Your wedding makes solemn what you've already done—the decision to love that you have pledged in many spoken and unspoken ways. In this chapter, I'd like to talk a little about a concept that may seem at first to be abstract, but which is, in fact, intended to be just about the most concrete element in our lives as Christians—the idea of *sacrament*.

For years Catholics memorized this definition of sacrament: "...an outward sign instituted by Christ to give grace." That's not a bad definition. As human beings, we all need signs. You will exchange wedding rings. You send flowers or cards to express your love. Most of us have some personal symbols special to us and to our relationships. All of these are ways to express what love means.

The same use of signs comes into play when we try to express our thoughts and beliefs about God. In a way, *who God is* is inexpressible. Try for a moment to describe God in a word. The concept tends to overload one's circuits!

In the language of the Old Testament, folks had a more colorful way of dealing with this problem. It was their belief that if you saw God face-to-face, you would die. Remember the climactic scene in *Raiders of the Lost Ark* when the Ark of the Covenant is opened? The rather messy fate of the Nazi soldiers in that special-effects masterpiece would have evoked understanding nods from the Hebrews who had trembled in the desert at the foot of Mt. Sinai.

God Gives Us a Living Sign of Love

Christianity is founded on the Good News that God has taken steps to overcome that gap between the human and the divine. We call the meeting between God and humanity the *Incarnation*. Another way of saying this is that God has become one of us in Jesus Christ. That *is* Good News! God could have arranged it some other way. I often speculate, being a science fiction fan, about some mystical meeting of minds, a sort of "mind meld" like *Star Trek*'s Mr. Spock was supposed to do.

But the basic truth of Christianity, the Incarnation, brings us into relationship with God in a way that is not alien to us, but truly human. Jesus Christ walked in a particular time and place with real people, people who were so captured by his message of love that they went on to lay their own lives on the line for that Good News.

The very presence of God in Jesus Christ is itself a sign, a sacrament. Jesus is the visible way, we believe, that we come to know God fully. The Church, the community of women and men who put faith in Jesus, has become a sign as well: the visible presence of Jesus in the world. So it is that others, searching for the unique truth that God became human, look to the Church to discover that revelation in the followers of Jesus. We—all of us—are that sign, that sacrament. The rest of the sacraments flow from those two fundamental sacraments.

Look at it this way: The two of you are, together, a sign of a new reality, you *as a couple*. You choose more specific signs to point to that relationship: You will send wedding invitations, have wedding portraits taken, exchange rings and so forth.

In the Church we have specific signs to express aspects of our life with God in Jesus Christ: the seven sacraments. To celebrate life, birth, belonging, growing, healing, loving, serving, dying; to mark the crucial moments of our lives; to identify special roles and relationships in our community—to do all this, the Church uses seven sacraments (Baptism, Confirmation, Eucharist, Reconciliation, Marriage, Ordination and Anointing of the Sick). These are, we believe, gifts from Jesus, preserved in our community as special, love-filled and powerful moments that express and create the meanings they embody.

Thus, at Baptism, we pour water. This beautiful rite carries meaning (washing, cleansing, bringing life). When done in a faith-context we believe it also *creates* what it symbolizes: It makes a person part of the mystery of Jesus as a member of the Church.

The same holds for the other sacraments as well, including the special sign you are now busy planning: the Sacrament of Marriage. Where the other sacraments use water, bread or oil, here too there is a visible, touchable, human element: the two of you bringing your whole selves to the ceremony.

You Are the Sign

You—your minds and hearts, hopes and desires, bodies and creative energies—become when joined together a sign of how God wants to be joined with the human family—and especially with the two of you, as part of your marriage relationship.

That is why we say that the two of you are really the *ministers* of the Sacrament of Marriage. The priest or deacon is merely an official witness for the Church community. You each give the sacrament to each other as you give yourselves to each other. As the priest or deacon says to you in the marriage ritual right before you exchange vows:

> My dear friends, you have come together in this church so that the Lord may seal and strengthen your love in the presence of the Church's minister and this community. Christ abundantly blesses this

love. He has already consecrated you in baptism and now he enriches and strengthens you by a special sacrament so that you may assume the duties of marriage in mutual and lasting fidelity. (*Rite of Marriage*, #23)

Through your sacrament, the two of you become the powerful sign of Christ's love for each other—*and* for the world. We all need the sign you become. We in the Church community are aware of the connection between your love and Christ's. In fact, we celebrate it with you in the religious ceremony—that's why the Church has cherished Jesus' understanding of marriage and calls it a sacrament.

We recognize that, as you draw upon God's presence as a "third party" in your relationship, your witness of love helps the community of believers as well. In you, the rest of us look to see God at work:

- God loves us in a binding, never-broken, permanent way. Your marriage must mirror that permanence.
- God is always faithful. You must be faithful to each other.
- God is good and gracious to us, forgiving and healing us. You must love and forgive each other.
- God's love has overflowed to create the world and all that is in it. You must bring new and creative life into our world.

We look to you to see God at work. You are a sacrament of God, and your sacrament, marriage, is a power-filled sign that goes on and on as long as you live. Understanding that reality is essential to planning your wedding liturgy.

What Do You Want for Your Wedding?

1) What special signs do you as a couple use to express
   your relationship?

2) What does the term *sacrament* mean for you?

3) What external symbols do you recall from other
   sacramental moments you have experienced in the
   Church?

4) Do you recall any especially good celebrations in Church? Any that were not as helpful to your faith?

5) How would you like your wedding to express what you believe: about God, about faith in Jesus Christ, about love, about each other, about your family and friends, about the community?

Chapter Three
The Church Wedding

C ouples confronting the task of planning a *church* wedding—with the rules and regulations a parish or diocese or the Church itself might require— may be tempted to ask, "Why bother with it all?" Having a church wedding means dealing with the "capital *C* " Church and all that comes with it.

To answer the question, I'd like to look at a church *building*—a parish church where I have often presided at Sunday Mass. This particular church, in a midwestern city, was built after Vatican II in a contemporary style of architecture. There are no stained-glass windows, very little decoration—in fact, the walls are dark gray poured concrete. Some people criticize this church for its starkness, its lack of "religious" appearance. They may be right: I am not an architect, and there are many tastes.

But from my perspective at the altar, as the presider on Sunday mornings, I witness something that makes the architect's plan for this building seem appropriate. As the pews fill up with people, my attention turns not to beautiful stained glass, mosaics or statues, but to what *really* makes a building a church: the people. There in all its variety is *the* Church, what Vatican II described as "the People of God."

Getting all those folks into church, settled for prayer, formed into a worshiping community involves some doing. To help, we may need a parking lot, a heating/air conditioning system, ushers, hymnals and so on—a lot of effort and expense.

And, when it all comes together, it is an assembly as varied as a garden full of wildflowers. There are the old and the young, liberal and conservative, awake and sleepy, eager and reluctant. It's complicated, confusing, annoying at times and occasionally even painful. It's not the most perfect gathering one might choose. But, for better or worse, it *is* the Church.

For better or worse—does that sound familiar? Well, there is a parallel. Whether it is the Sunday assembly of your parish or the two of you preparing for marriage, we are still talking about *people*. It's people who make up the Church.

Human Relationships: A Model for Relating to God

But how do we get from the typical Sunday congregation to the two of you, sitting at a kitchen table, writing wedding invitations? How do you fit into Church? And how does your wedding—and the marriage that flows from it—get to be a "Church" concern?

It begins—again—with people.

I like to take anything that has to do with God or religion or Church back to human relationships. There, we find a pattern for relating to God. Look at any human friendship that enriches your life. Look at the positive, challenging, growth-nurturing experiences of relating to another. Look at the relationship which the two of you share today. There, I believe, we can find a model for that deep dimension of our lives which we label "religious."

That's not a new thought. It's as old as our Judeo-Christian religion itself, which has two great commandments: one about loving God and another about loving neighbor as oneself. Jesus saw these two as parts of one commandment—so much so that he told the enduring story of an outsider who stopped along the road to help a traveler in distress when others had passed by. For Jesus, the Good Samaritan's behavior toward a fellow human being became the measure for a relationship to God (see Luke 10:29-37).

How does a friend relate to us—listening, understanding, forgiving, challenging? The answer to the question might describe how God has loved us. What

22

do we give in return to a friend—affirmation, gratitude, a wish for growth? The answer to that question can tell us how we might relate to God.

Simple enough. The "friendship model" isn't just descriptive, however. It also helps us to understand some of the more puzzling aspects of relating to God. Prayer, for example.

If prayer is like talking to a friend, then almost anything that happens in our human communication might turn up—at least from our side—when we talk to God. If God seems silent when you pray, how have you felt when a friend listens silently to your tale of woe? Perhaps both God and your friend would rather listen supportively than give answers.

The human institution we call *Church* may be for you another puzzling aspect of things religious. Why go through all of the paperwork, the legalities of a Church wedding, the ritual, the rules about music, time and place, wedding vows? Some couples planning a wedding—especially if they have not been active in Church for a while—may see these things as a thick forest, something to struggle through.

Think again of human relationships, especially your own. When you first fell in love, it was between the two of you. It may have been very private, very personal, a special secret sharing. Who else knows you? Who else makes the world sing, even on a cloudy day? Who finally understands what you've been trying to say and do all these years?

Relationships begin there, in the intimate circle that bonds two people together. But they don't stay there. Soon you wanted to share the joy you were feeling with other friends, confidants, your parents. You brought him or her home to meet the folks. You wanted your buddies to get to know her, your girlfriends to see how special he is.

That intimate circle began to expand. It stretched to take in a much wider circle—including those who are part of other relationships, other circles.

Eventually, for those who take the step of marriage, the relationship becomes a formal one. It is recognized by civil authorities and, in the same logical expansion of relationships, by the circle of relationships we call *Church*.

Rituals Strengthen Relationships

When that expansion first takes place, certain customs and rules begin to operate. Whom did you tell first about your new love? Probably something inside of you led you to a best friend. Or, if family loyalty and ties are important for you, you shared it with Mom or Dad.

When your relationship became more serious, perhaps family custom dictated a dinner with the in-laws. You began to see wider circles and knew that you must do certain things—*rituals*, we call them—to ensure that the bonds that form those circles stay strong.

Finally, as you formally decided to become engaged, even more customs and rules took hold: You had to inform coworkers and employers; friends wanted to plan showers, and so on. Eventually you touched such mundane but necessary circles as those that link you to the IRS, Social Security, the courthouse, the real estate agent.

Do you begin to see a pattern? The details of wedding planning that involve the Church are a part of that pattern, begun when the two of you first shared a special moment together. The Church, like the other institutions of family or state, has its own customs, rules, traditions—and *rituals*. In the Church, we use these rituals (and all the rest) to keep intact the bonds that unite us.

Thus, for centuries Christians have gathered to eat a meal and tell the story of Jesus. Why? Because we know that meal—the Eucharist—carries more than just ordinary nourishment. It is an act of unity, a moment of powerful bonding. There, in a human sign, we meet God and are brought more closely in union with each other.

If, soon after Jesus' time, the sign (eating and

drinking) had been changed to something else, then changed again and again, it would have lost its value as a sign. We do not lightly tamper with such things. Imagine suggesting that you *not* bring out Grandma's best china for those special family meals or altering the way Christmas Eve is celebrated, or passing up Cousin George's annual family reunion picnic!

The rituals, rules and customs we have in the Church function the same way. We in the community have agreed on them from year to year, finding them helpful to us in bringing home special meanings and memories. Rituals enshrine values and form the sacramental context in which we continue actively to remember and celebrate Jesus Christ.

All the customs and rules surrounding a Church wedding may still seem strange. Why, for example, do you have to deal with a parish? Can't you just have the wedding in a pretty setting, even outdoors? Why do you have to relate to this particular priest, the pastor (especially if his personality and yours clash)? Why can't you simply make your own choices?

Those are good questions; many couples have them. Church weddings do have a lot to do with a real church building and the real people who populate it. That's because buildings and parish boundaries and flesh-and-blood individuals (even pastors!) are our human way of *locating* the more intangible parts of what we understand as Church. This localizing (or perhaps even "sacramentalizing") is akin to what we discussed in the last chapter.

When we come to the complicated relationships that make up a family or any other human group, we need concrete ways to deal with them. Families have reunions, old homesteads (or pictures of them), patriarchs and matriarchs. Other groups have clubhouses, meeting rooms, corporate headquarters. Countries have capitals. We need to *ground* the otherwise tentative bonds that hold human groups together.

That's why we have parishes: They "localize" the

Church. They give us a place where smaller groups can meet and various cultural expressions can be celebrated. The church building becomes the visible sign of that local group. For many Catholics, it is a powerful sign.

I recall my home parish in Cincinnati. Crucial to the history of our parish was the fact that parishioners actually dug the church's foundations by hand when a building contractor refused to tackle the tough clay. That communal action inspired me years later, when I read about it in the parish history. Without the visible sign of the towering church building and the knowledge of how it got there, my understanding of the "spiritual" dimension of *Church* would have been so much poorer.

True, sometimes the sign isn't so great. We may disagree about church architecture or how to pay for a new church building. You may find your home parish less than suitable for your wedding either physically or emotionally. And yet, it *is* where we begin—for there Christians gather and celebrate the memories that bring them together.

(If you discover that neither of your home parishes "works" for whatever reason, you can discuss this with the one who is assisting you in wedding planning. Usually that is something you do in the early stages of arranging a wedding in the Church.)

Ritual Can Involve Choices

Not all ritual, rules or customs have equal weight. That is, in part, what this book is all about—helping you sort through them. You have choices, just as the community has had through the ages. Some customs *do* change; some rituals may not always work. Aunt Rita's old 1950's electric roaster may be an antique, but a modern oven may cook the Thanksgiving turkey a lot better. In my family, however, that venerable appliance still does a great job, according to my mother. It all comes down to choices!

Vatican II, with its renewal of Church liturgy (its

"ritual life"), brought about some changes in the way we do all the sacraments. Marriage was no exception. Liturgists studied marriage rituals down through the years. They rewrote texts, added new ones based on the rich history of theology and practice and recognized that people need options and flexibility.

Couples now have some flexibility in choosing a parish church for the wedding ceremony. You can probably invite a priest or deacon of your choosing to take part. You have the freedom to look over the structure of the wedding liturgy and make choices.

Whatever you choose for your wedding liturgy, know that you are involved in shaping the bonds that link you into the Church community. In a real way, you are strengthening your relationship with God, in and through the people who will share your wedding day with you. The care you take with your planning will be as important as the many other details you are attending to as you plan a lifetime together.

What Do You Want for Your Wedding?

1) What does *family* mean for you? How do family ties function in your life?

2) Have you ever thought of your parish or the Church as a family?

3) How important to you are the traditions of your family? Of the Church?

4) How do you define *Church*?

5) Do you identify with a particular church building?
   What associations does it have for you?

6) Describe the church where your wedding will be held.
   Why have you chosen it?

Chapter Four

Narrowing Your Choices: The Structure of the Rite

F or me, one of the best parts of dining in a good restaurant is looking at the menu. Even though I know I can't have all the choices, the fun is in looking over the appetizers, entrees and desserts and imagining what each might taste like. I bring a lot to that experience: previous meals, a sense of adventure, wanting to make "healthy" choices and sometimes just splurging.

In the last chapter, we began talking about the choices that face you in planning your wedding. Now, it's time we looked at the menu—not for the rehearsal dinner or the reception, however, but the "main course": your wedding *liturgy*.

What exactly goes into a wedding liturgy? How does it all fit together? On pages 81 to 85 you will find two planning guides—one for the liturgy, another for wedding music. They represent the "menu." They will give you a chance to specify the elements that will go into your wedding. As you go through the rest of this book, you'll learn more about some of the major parts or elements, and a lot of detail about the little items. Before we get around to ordering, let's look at the major parts of this "wedding menu" and how they fit together.

The Structure Helps It Flow

A good meal has a structure that lends to the dining experience: The appetizer leads to the salad, and then on to the entree and finally dessert. Just so, the wedding liturgy has a structure that helps one element flow into another. Being aware of structure and flow can lead you to a well-planned, joyful celebration that will express your faith and commitment.

There are five major parts to the wedding liturgy, four if you choose *not* to have your wedding in the context of a Mass. Corresponding to each of these parts is a purpose, which helps that part relate to the rest of the liturgy. The five parts and their purposes are as follows:

1) *The Entrance Rite*: Here music begins, guests arrive, the wedding party enters and greetings are exchanged between the presiding minister, the couple and the congregation. The purpose of this part is to *set a mood*. Guests have time to arrive and assume an attentive, prayerful attitude; the members of the wedding party enter formally and present themselves, arrayed in their wedding best, to the assembly.

There is a moment of transition from the entrance procession, as guests watch and pictures are taken, to respectful listening as the Scriptures are proclaimed.

2) *The Liturgy of the Word*: The readings from the Word of God are proclaimed, the assembly listens and responds. The presider reflects on the Word and the occasion in the homily. The purpose of this part is to help us *understand the seriousness of the moment* when two people commit their lives to one another.

3) *The Rite of Marriage*: The couple declare their intention to marry, solemnly state their consent and exchange rings. There may also be other ceremonies here, such as the lighting of a wedding candle. This is a "peak moment," whose purpose is sacramental: *two people become, in the presence of the Church, a sign of God's love in their lives and in ours*. The moment is marked by an outpouring of joy and thanks.

When marriage is celebrated without a Mass (in cases where the bride and groom come from two different faith expressions), the Rite of Marriage includes special petitions, a nuptial blessing and the Lord's Prayer. Where Eucharist will follow, the Rite of Marriage ends with petitions, just as at Sunday Mass.

4) *The Liturgy of the Eucharist*: When marriage is celebrated with a Mass, the altar table is prepared, gifts are brought forth and the Eucharistic Prayer is proclaimed. We pray the Lord's Prayer and a special nuptial blessing prior to sharing in Communion.

This part of the liturgy follows one "peak moment" with another—a dramatic time of praise and thanksgiving in the context of Jesus' dying and rising as celebrated in the eucharistic banquet. The purpose (at least in relation to your wedding) is to *parallel the unity of the newly married couple with the unity between Jesus and the Church.*

5) *The Dismissal Rite*: In either type of wedding (with or without Mass), we conclude with another blessing and a procession out, leading to the rest of the wedding festivities. The purpose here is to *bring closure to one stage of the wedding and lead to what follows*—not only the wedding reception, but the rest of your lives.

How to 'Place Your Order'

Knowing what to order from a restaurant menu makes all the difference in the meal. You wouldn't normally choose two entrees or three desserts. Tastes, balanced diet, pocketbook—a number of criteria help you make up your mind. Once you have an idea of what kind of meal you are ready for, you can really begin studying the menu.

That's what the planning guides on pages 81 to 85 will help you to do. You don't have to fill them in completely at this point. Some of the items may be clear; others may need explanation. In the rest of this book, detailed explanations will help you to understand the particular parts.

For now, just look over the planning guides to get the "big picture" once more. If you have particular questions, note them to discuss with each other, your priest or deacon or the married couple who is assisting you.

In the next two chapters, we'll explore two aspects of your wedding that deserve special attention: the

Scripture readings and the music. The choices you have there are enough, you will discover, to satisfy those who enjoy attending to details.

What Do You Want for Your Wedding?

Look over the planning guides (pages 81 to 85). Make note of those items about which you want to ask questions.

Chapter Five

Telling God's Story and Yours: The Scriptures

In J.R.R. Tolkien's classic fantasy trilogy *The Lord of the Rings*, the hero, Frodo the hobbit, and his companion, Sam, undertake a perilous quest to destroy the Ring of Power, a quest which leads them into great dangers. At one particularly difficult moment, the two characters pause along their way to rest. As they eat a sparse meal and prepare to move on, Sam remarks how he feels that he has "fallen into a tale"—a story a parent might read to a child, years later, out of a book. He and Frodo chuckle at the thought, then shiver as they realize that at "this point someone might say, 'Shut the book now, Dad; we don't want to read any more.' "

That brief moment from a gripping tale illustrates a deeper truth: We are *all* in a story. The story is our own.

You know that already, as you begin to build one life together out of two. I'm sure that as a couple, your *new* story is already assuming a definite shape. Special moments, future plans, even arguments make up the story.

A friend of mine, newly engaged, not long ago invited me to an evening at which she, her fiancé and some friends were going to commemorate the night they first met. We were all to meet at the same local pub and recreate that special moment. It was special because it was the first scene in a developing story.

Stories are a crucial part of human life. Theologian John Shea says, "We are born into a community of stories and storytellers." He goes on to link human stories to what he calls "the stories of God."

We all know *those* stories. We find them in the pages

of the Bible. In planning your wedding, you will open that collection of God-stories. There, you will choose several "pages" that will mark the sacramental beginning of your own story as a couple.

God's Stories Are Also Our Story

The Bible may present a unique problem for a couple faced with choosing wedding readings. Most of us know something about the Bible. We can probably relate a few—perhaps many—stories from its pages. But, apart from the familiar tales of Adam and Eve and Moses and stories about Jesus, the Bible may be an imposing minefield of strange names, seemingly endless lists of archaic laws and some pretty tough theology. And it *is* all of those things! But it is more.

That "more" is what I consider the truly *easy* aspect of the Sacred Scriptures. If we can look beyond the obvious historical and theological problems the Bible presents to a reader, we might begin to see that it was written by people like ourselves. True, the biblical authors (and there were more than one) came from different cultures, wrote in different languages and lived in different times. But they were *human* like us and faced similar human situations.

When we read their stories—like that of Adam and Eve, wrestling with good and evil; or Moses, seeking with his people a special relationship with God; or Jesus, seated on a mountaintop, explaining in terms of sheep, lost coins and buried treasure, how God's love was breaking into human life—we are reading *our own story*. Isn't it true that *we* wrestle with good and evil, and sometimes—as a youngster in a religion class explained to me once—bite into a "poisoned apple"? Don't we long for a relationship with God, despite the fact that we may have to endure a trip through a "desert" to find it? And doesn't God's love break into your life and mine in such everyday ways? Maybe not in sheep or buried treasures, but perhaps through softball games, backyard cookouts

36

or a late-night trip to the emergency room.

Scripture is about us as much as it is about God. To quote my Franciscan colleague again: "The Bible is simply the story of God saying, 'I love you,' to the human family, as well as the story of our response to God in return."

Choosing Scriptures That Tell Your Story

Of the various parts of the wedding liturgy, the Liturgy of the Word is the one that ought to receive your first and best attention. It consists, usually, of three main Scripture passages, one chosen from the Old Testament and two selections from the New—one from the Gospels and one from the section of the New Testament where the "letters" are found.

A fourth bit of Scripture can be chosen from the Old Testament Book of Psalms to serve as a response to the first (Old Testament) selection. You may, however, opt for a *song* to sing in response to the first reading. (More about that in the next chapter.)

How do you choose? Where do you look for appropriate selections? The best way to settle on the Scripture readings for your wedding is with prayer. You might even want to make the process of choosing part of a simple prayer service (see the suggestion at the end of this chapter).

The Church has done some of the work for you already. There is a list of 28 possible readings (in addition to the psalm responses) from which to choose. These represent key passages from Scripture which relate marriage to the larger context of God saying "I love you" to the human family. (The full texts of these readings can be found in Appendix A; see page 87.)

Although most couples restrict their choice of Scripture readings to those listed in the wedding ritual, some may want to use other selections from the Bible. The ritual itself seems to leave that possibility open, noting simply that the listed readings "may be used."

Discuss this possibility with your priest or deacon if you have other favorite Bible passages—making sure, of course, that they harmonize with your wedding theme and are not simply favorite texts that do not relate.

Couples sometimes ask about using nonbiblical readings in a wedding. The basic rule of thumb is that the Liturgy of the Word is reserved for the Scriptures. If you have other favorite poems or texts you would like as part of your liturgy, there are ways this can be done. They might find a place in an introductory welcoming statement, in a brief meditation after the wedding vows or in a post-Communion meditation.

Be wary, however, of adding more words to the liturgy. Let the signs and symbols speak for themselves. The power and poetry of the Scriptures, a few well-chosen reflections and your own statement of consent may be all the words you need. Consider using that favorite poem or quote at the wedding rehearsal or rehearsal dinner as part of a brief time of prayer. Or print it in the wedding program (with appropriate permission, if needed).

A Guide to the Scripture Selections

Your priest or deacon is a resource for you in choosing the Scriptures. He will reflect on them as part of his homily or sermon at the end of the Liturgy of the Word, right before you exchange your wedding vows. So it might be good to involve him as much as possible in your choices.

Over the years, I've watched many couples choose their readings. My own wedding preaching has grown and developed largely as a result of their choices. I'd like to share some insights those choices have evoked in me as a guide to your own selection process.

In most wedding planning guides (including Appendix A of this book), you will find the wedding readings listed in biblical order—as they can be found in the Bible, from front to back. Here, however, I'd like to propose a different grouping based on my experience in preaching at weddings, which may be helpful. My listing falls into four categories: (1) the "all-time favorites," (2) the "good sermon-starters," (3) the "culturally difficult" and (4) the "risk-takers."

It admittedly sounds like a subjective listing, but I offer it as a help to you and to the priest or deacon who will share your wedding liturgy with you.

The All-Time Favorites

1) Genesis 2:18-24
2) Tobit 8:5-7
3) Song of Songs 2:8-10, 14, 16a; 8:6-7a
4) 1 Corinthians 12:31—13:8
5) Colossians 3:12-17
6) 1 John 4:7-12
7) Matthew 19:3-6
8) Mark 10:6-9
9) John 15:9-12
10) John 15:12-16
11) John 17:20-26 or 20-23

In this group of Scripture selections you will find those you've probably heard at the weddings of your friends. They are most often chosen by couples nowadays.

Included here are the story of the creation of man and woman (1); Jesus' saying about the unity of husband and wife (7, 8); three selections about love from the Gospel of John (9, 10, 11); three other New Testament selections on love (4, 5, 6), including the "all-time top vote-getter" among wedding readings—Paul's explanation of love from 1 Corinthians. Finally, there are two recent favorites I have begun to hear more often: the story of Tobiah and Sarah on their wedding night (2) and a love poem from the Old Testament Song of Songs (3).

Why pick readings from this group? Well, the popularity of these readings among wedding couples seems to indicate that the liturgists who drew up the list of Scripture selections were on target for couples in the modern United States with nearly half their choices. These readings seem to touch commonly agreed-upon themes of love and how it is lived out in marriage. Contained here, too, are some of the biblical texts best known even outside of wedding liturgies. You can't go wrong making choices from this group, experience seems to indicate.

On the other hand, in settling for readings so often heard, you may be missing an opportunity. Going beyond the popular choices may lead you into some new Scriptural discoveries and may open the ears of those who will celebrate with you at your wedding liturgy.

The Good Sermon-Starters

1) Jeremiah 31:31-32a, 33-34a
2) Romans 12:1-2, 9-18 or 1-2, 9-13
3) Matthew 5:1-12
4) Matthew 5:13-16
5) Matthew 7:21, 24-29 or 21, 24-25
6) Matthew 22:35-40

In this group (a really subjective gathering), I've put readings that I find easy to preach from at weddings. The Jeremiah reading (1) is one I will most often suggest to couples if they ask me for an Old Testament choice. I like the idea of God doing something new in us, by writing a covenant "in our hearts."

Here, too, is my favorite wedding Gospel—the Beatitudes (3). Perhaps my affection for it comes from an experience I had once, which I'll save for the end of this chapter. Suffice it to say here that the Beatitudes, along with the other selections from Matthew about the salt of the earth (4), building on rock (5) or the two great commandments (6) make good places to begin talking about the realities of married life and love. So does the Romans reading (2), which is a fresh alternative to the frequently used Corinthians reading about love.

Your wedding preacher may disagree with me or add other selections. I simply offer mine here as another way to discuss what might help that preacher reflect with you and your guests on the meaning of marriage.

The Culturally Difficult

1) Tobit 7:9-10, 11-15
2) Sirach 26:1-4, 13-16
3) Ephesians 5:2a, 21-33 or 2a, 25-32
4) 1 Peter 3:1-9

Each book of the Bible was written in a specific place, time and culture. Therefore, in addition to being the Word of God, the Bible also contains many *human* expressions of that Word. Some of those expressions may be from a culture very different than ours.

Included in the selections for wedding liturgies are four such readings. The Tobit reading (1) depicts Tobiah's choice of his wife Sarah being negotiated in the cultural situation of the time, in which a woman married within a certain tribe and was given in marriage by contract. Hidden in verse 11 is a beautiful expression of loving and being loved, but the surrounding verses may require more explanation than can be done adequately in a wedding homily.

The same applies to the two New Testament selections (3, 4) which reflect cultural conditions of the time, in which wives were subject to their husbands. The scriptural truth behind these conditioned words is that the husband is to love his wife *as Christ loved us*, that is, selflessly. Such a love is far from oppressive. But getting to that explanation again takes time.

Finally, the Sirach reading (2) concentrates only on the qualities of a "good wife," and may lead some to conclude that the woman is being described only in relation to what she can do for her husband. Again, the truth behind the words focuses elsewhere: Here is one path to holiness. But that truth needs to be explained.

Isolating these readings as "culturally difficult" is not to demean them. It merely is a warning to you that Scripture can't always be read or used without

41

explanation. It is up to you and your priest or deacon to consider how much explanation is appropriate in the wedding homily. If you choose any of these readings—and you may have excellent reasons to do so—be sure that you help your listeners *truly* to appreciate them.

The Risk-Takers
1) Genesis 1:26-28, 31a
2) Genesis 24:48-51, 58-67
3) Romans 8:31b-35, 37-39
4) 1 Corinthians 6:13c-15a, 17-20
5) 1 John 3:18-24
6) Revelation 19:1, 5-9a
7) John 2:1-11

In this group, I've arbitrarily placed readings that I have almost never heard used in wedding liturgies. To me, they represent a challenge—to the couple choosing them, to the preacher and to the listeners. Look at some of the interesting possibilities (and consider the potential difficulties) offered in these selections:

The first Genesis reading (1) tells a creation story that might present a complement to another of this group, the Corinthians reading (4). The earthiness of the first creation story and the acceptance of ourselves as "body-persons" could lead to a reflection on how sexuality expresses God's wonderful and challenging creation of us all.

The other Genesis reading (2) may at first seem caught up in culture, but also features Rebecca's choice of Isaac, given a culturally conditioned arrangement. It could lead to reflections on the challenging roles of women and men in marriage today in the context of God's action in choosing us.

The Romans reading (3) dwells on the hardships that may lie in the future—perhaps a challenge for all to hear on the happy occasion of a wedding. The reading from John's letter (5) could be another fresh reflection on what love means, again in terms of what Jesus did for us in dying on the cross.

The story of the wedding feast at Cana (7) was the *only* choice for years in the pre-Vatican II wedding Mass. Preachers may want to attempt to give it a fresh look for use in today's weddings.

Finally, the Revelation selection (6) about the wedding feast of the Lamb offers an opportunity for a symbolic comparison of your marriage with the "marriage" between Christ and the Church.

Now It's Up to You

My reflections and those of your priest or deacon, along with Scripture guides or commentaries, can assist you in choosing your wedding readings. In the end, it comes back to your own story. The creative choices you make will depend on how you see your story fitting into the larger story of how God has loved the human family, especially in the gift of Jesus.

Jesus' relationship to us in the Church, as highlighted in some of the readings noted above, has traditionally formed a theological base for understanding Christian marriage. That insight, whether you choose those particular readings or not, can help you in relating your story to God's. And that's where a particular story of mine, promised earlier, may help.

A number of years ago, two friends planning their wedding chose the Gospel of the Beatitudes (Matthew 5:3-12) as one of their readings. The words, they said, expressed how they felt about their marriage. There, Jesus tells of the blessings of the "reign of God": "Blessed are the poor in spirit.... Blessed are the meek.... Blessed are the peacemakers...." I also felt the text was appropriate. The Beatitudes are a "blueprint" for a marriage—a way to look at a life filled with many unknowns. My friends wished to proclaim, "We want to live our life in this way."

The words they chose were truer than they knew. Later that year I heard that my friends were expecting

43

their first child. During her pregnancy, the mother-to-be found time to reflect on what having a baby meant. She wrote a letter to the editor of the local paper, telling how her unborn child seemed to be showing her that all life was precious and needed to be safeguarded.

Then one night I got a phone call at three a.m. My friends' child—a little girl—had died as she was being born. At the hospital, I shared the sadness of these parents as they said good-bye to their child. We met later to talk about the funeral liturgy for the infant. My friends had obviously prayed and thought about what they wanted to do. They told me that they wanted to use the same Gospel for the funeral as they had used for their wedding: the Beatitudes.

Now, they said, they really understood what those words of Jesus meant, especially, "Blessed are they who mourn..." (Matthew 5:4a). They knew that life held both joys and sorrows, and still they kept faith. They understood better now than on their wedding day that Jesus was present with them no matter what happened, helping them to see even this moment of deep sorrow and grief as "blessed."

You, I hope, will never have to recall your wedding readings in quite so dramatic a fashion. But the choices you make now ought to have a meaning that will last throughout your marriage, as my friends' did.

What Do You Want for Your Wedding?

Use this informal prayer service to accompany your choice of wedding Scripture selections.

Alone together or with your priest or deacon, begin with a moment of silence. Ask God, in words of your own choosing, to open you to the richness of the Word. Imagine how God might speak to you through the passages you will read and study together. Then, read several of them aloud, slowly and thoughtfully. As you read, pause and share with each other what you think the reading is saying. Ask yourselves:

44

- How might this reading possibly be about *us* as a couple?
- Does anything special strike me?
- Do any of the words carry a special impact?
- Do the incidents in the stories or the themes expressed find an echo in our relationship?

The answers to these questions can help you narrow your choices. If each of you has different choices, that's OK. As you discuss and compromise, you shape your new story as a couple. God is at work through you *as a couple*, and your religious insights will grow out of a shared spirituality. Let that process begin!

Chapter Six

Ten Tips About Choosing Wedding Music

M usic plays a big part in most weddings. Music enhances the celebration and creates a beautiful mood. It's where weddings begin and end—with the procession up the aisle and the last song at the reception.

Most of us have music we like. Our preferences may vary widely, but we all tune to a particular station on our car radios or collect cassettes or CDs of our favorite groups. Your taste may be helpful in instructing the band or DJ for your wedding reception, but in planning the program of wedding music to be used in church, you may face a dilemma: You may not be familiar with Church music. The parish or priest may have rules about what can be sung. You may not know a liturgical musician.

In this chapter, I'd like to borrow on the expertise of a musician who has played and planned many weddings to offer you ten suggestions for becoming at least temporary experts in the field of wedding music.

1) Seek Out a Competent Musician

Who will play the music and lead the singing at your wedding? Couples sometimes have a friend who "has a good voice." Even though you may have enjoyed his or her ability to make music, *planning* wedding music may be another matter.

The same principle goes for the parish folk group. You may enjoy their musical leadership at Sunday Mass, but check on their experience with weddings. If it's limited, you may need to look elsewhere.

So where *do* you look? Your parish music director
(even though you may not eventually choose him or her)
is a good person to start with. Music directors always
have collections of liturgically appropriate selections;
often they keep copies of wedding music programs and
can share what others have done. They also can help you
negotiate with pastors and parishes in regard to local
guidelines.

You may also want to inquire among your friends or of
the priest or deacon helping you with the rest of your
wedding plans. They often know of groups or individuals
who specialize in playing weddings. If you are an
interfaith couple, be sure and consult musicians from
both of your faith-traditions, so that your final program
can reflect the musical richness those traditions
embrace.

2) Get a List of Wedding Music

Don't just say, "I heard this song on the radio that I like."
Not all music is appropriate for weddings. The suitability
of music depends on a number of factors—not all of them
immediately apparent. To begin with, the words may
express themes that clash with the values of our
faith-community or the melody may not convey a spirit
that is helpful for prayer.

Granted, such judgments are often subjective.
Nevertheless, people make them. In fact, some parishes
have guidelines for what music can be played at
weddings. Again, a competent church musician may be
your best resource. Some parishes provide a list of
acceptable songs for you along with other premarital
planning materials when you make your reservation for
your wedding.

Another criterion for appropriate music is artistic
merit. Being "secular" or "religious" does not
automatically make a selection musically good. There are
good and bad in both categories. Once more, your
musician is an excellent resource for you in this area.

48

A listing of musical selections can help you understand what songs are appropriate for weddings. A couple may suggest James Taylor's "Fire and Rain," for example. It's a beautiful song, but the words refer to someone dying—how appropriate is that for a wedding?

Sometimes a song from the Top 40 may be quite suitable in connection with a wedding. Given the particular guidelines of your parish, your musician may use it as a meditation or in a prelude medley. Most secular songs, however, will not work as a response to a reading or during the distribution of Communion.

At the end of this chapter, you'll find a list of questions you can ask about music choices you may be considering. Those questions will help you judge the appropriateness of specific songs and other musical selections.

3) Sit Down Together as a Couple and Talk

Recently a bride-to-be came to a planning session with her mother and father. The groom-to-be didn't come. There obviously had been no planning; she had no idea what her fiancé wanted. You need to reflect together on what theme you want expressed and what kind of music you like (secular and religious). Are you traditional? Do you prefer more contemporary music?

If you come from different faith-traditions, doing this planning may be more of a challenge. A Catholic may know "On Eagles' Wings" (a modern liturgical song popular at many Catholic parishes), while his or her partner may not be familiar with that popular hymn. The same will be true for the rich repertoire of hymns from the rest of the Christian community. But unless you talk together, you won't be creating a program that truly reflects the unity you hope to celebrate at your wedding.

4) Let the Music Flow From the Scripture Readings

The Scriptures will aid you in narrowing your criteria for musical choices. In the poetry of the Bible, you'll find words that are echoed in both liturgical and secular songs. The popular song "Longer" (a Top 40 hit by Dan Fogelberg) seems to flow from the *covenant* theme found in the reading from Jeremiah we highlighted in the last chapter. In "Longer," the singer describes a loving commitment in terms of the ageless stars in the sky—a comparison to be found in the way the Bible talks about God's covenant with humanity.

In parish hymnals—both folk and more traditional—you will find many biblically based songs. Often a hymnal will even group wedding songs together in an index. Paging through the song books you find in the pews is not a bad way to learn about appropriate wedding music.

The readings you will select for your liturgy will offer opportunities for a thematic approach to your music as well as a "musical" way to respond. Many psalm-based hymns can fulfill that function—for example, as mentioned in the last chapter, a suitable song can replace the Responsorial Psalm after the first reading.

5) Know Your Congregation

It's one thing to get a group of nonsingers to chime in for "Happy Birthday" at a party. It's another to expect a mixed group assembled in church for a wedding to sound like the Mormon Tabernacle Choir. Before you raise your expectations about the kind of music you pick for your wedding, think about who will be attending. Remember that most wedding congregations come from a variety of parishes and will never before have sung together in this particular church. They probably do not know the same songs. There may be a good number who don't attend church regularly, much less a Catholic ceremony.

In addition, at a wedding the guests are watching a beautiful bride and handsome groom take an important step in life. That preoccupation may distract guests from the kind of participation which includes singing. It may even frustrate you from the altar, as the two of you watch a well-planned musical program end up as a solo performance by your musicians.

If you are bringing together people from two different faith-expressions, you have a further need: to harmonize two distinct singing traditions. For example, members of other Christian Churches sing more than Catholics do and use a different repertoire of music. You will want to be sensitive and inclusive in that situation.

Knowing who will be in attendance will help you choose how much *singing* and how much *listening* you can reasonably expect.

6) Pick 'Singable' Music

"Singable" applies both to the musicians and the congregation. You may have heard a stirring rendition of "O Promise Me" at a friend's wedding. But if *your* musician can't handle it, you'd better choose something else.

From the congregation's side, hymns at weddings ought to be easy to sing, given the circumstances mentioned above. Ease in singing means simple melodies played in a range most people can reach. Drawing from familiar church music (if you know your congregation) can help here, too.

Despite the difficulties of getting a wedding congregation to sing, a few simple sung refrains, strategically placed, printed in a program and rehearsed at some point before the service begins can do wonders toward giving people a sense of togetherness.

One way to encourage participation (in addition to picking singable songs) is to invite a relative or friend who is comfortable speaking before people to come up to the front of church before the wedding procession and offer a word of welcome on your behalf. He or she can also encourage the guests to pray and sing, and can direct them to participation aids (a printed program or the parish hymnals). The song leader or your presider may be a substitute if you cannot find another person to fulfill this task.

7) Know When to Sing

Singing is one form of participation—the active kind. If you have thought about your congregation and feel that your musician can encourage them to take part, then you may want to choose some moments to emphasize in participatory song. Knowing *when* are the best moments to sing at a wedding liturgy is important. Here are some key times (not in order of importance):

A *"gathering song"*: after the wedding party has processed in, a singable hymn brings the assembly together in a shared moment of participation.

The Responsorial Psalm breaks up the readings nicely. After the first (Old Testament) reading, there is a sung response and then another (New Testament) reading. There are many beautiful psalm-based responsorial songs in hymnals or other collections. Have the congregation respond with the refrain of such a song— that's *active* participation—and, at the same time, listen to the verses—a more *passive* way of participating.

The Gospel Acclamation, a short, joyful burst of "Alleluia!" comes after the second (New Testament) reading and before the Gospel. Again, the congregation sings a refrain, and the musicians a verse. This acclamation should be sung; it's better to omit it rather than read it.

The Eucharistic Prayer acclamations are among the most important things to sing at any Mass, including a wedding Mass. These acclamations during the prayer that recalls what Jesus did at the Last Supper include the "Holy, Holy," the Memorial Acclamation in the middle of the prayer ("Christ has died...") and the "Great Amen" at the end of the prayer. Choose melodies familiar to the greatest number of people in the congregation; your musician can help in this.

Before and during Communion, you can sing the "Lamb of God" and a good singable eucharistic hymn. These help as people are receiving Communion to center us in on the mystery of Jesus nourishing us in his Body and Blood. I *don't* recommend singing the Lord's Prayer, although it is popular to suggest that a soloist sing it at weddings. This is a communal prayer and having everyone pray it together is the *first* emphasis. Also, a special Nuptial Blessing accompanies it at weddings and that can complicate a sung Lord's Prayer. And some of the sung versions popular in Catholic liturgy may not be familiar to all in your congregation.

8) Know When to Listen

As mentioned above, participation can also be *passive* in a positive sense. There are times when *listening* can be a prayerful, unifying experience. Some times to do this at wedding liturgies are:

Before the wedding, as guests are coming into church, can be a time for either "religious" or "secular" music. The purpose here is to set a mood of quiet and prayer. If an instrumental processional is used with a sung opening, however, be sure they complement each other.

The verses of a psalm response or the Gospel, as explained above.

During the preparation of the bread and wine at a wedding Mass. This is a time when attention is shifting from one part of the liturgy to another, a good time to listen.

After Communion some reflective time helps to make the transition to the dismissal.

During other wedding ceremonies which you may choose to add to your liturgy: the dedication to the Blessed Virgin Mary or a candle ceremony. (The next chapter will explain some of these customs and how they may be appropriately chosen).

9) Have Your Plans in Mind When You Meet Your Musician

Before you come to the music planning session, choose your readings and reflect on them. Also bring with you a good idea of what special customs and ceremonies you will include (see Chapter Seven).

Don't ask the musician to decide for you whether to include a particular custom or to help you choose the readings. Have your theme, your "flow," your ideas on paper when you meet to discuss music. These elements will dictate the song choices.

Also have the criteria discussed above—your style of music, the demands of your faith-tradition and so forth—in mind as you come to the meeting. The musician can then center in on the task of selecting from the repertoire what he or she knows will be appropriate for *your* wedding.

It will help, too, if you are ready to be realistic. Church musicians sometimes must "just say no" to a particular song that the couple may ask for. A song like "Holy God" may just not fit at Communion time, when a more meditative song that speaks of the Eucharist works better. If you really do want a song, ask *why* the musician thinks otherwise. In the process, some compromise may appear possible.

10) Don't Be Afraid to Be Creative

You've probably heard Paul Stookey's "Wedding Song" at countless liturgies. By now, many church musicians and couples consider it an overused song. When you come to make *your* choices, look at the wide range of music available to make your wedding a personal expression of faith and love.

Explore some different and creative alternatives: A beautiful instrumental on harp, oboe or cello might set a mood before the wedding or at another meditative time. Combine both organ and guitar selections. Use a classical guitarist to provide a meditation. Use the "gathering song" mentioned above.

Don't just get caught in what you've seen—like one bride who came in with five wedding programs, spread them out and said, "I don't know which of these to choose for my wedding!" The musician's first impulse was to say, "Throw them all away and let's be creative with *your* wedding."

What Do You Want for Your Wedding?

A special music planning guide can be found on pages 84 and 85. These questions from Jeremy Harrington's *Your Wedding* make a good test for any musical selection being considered for a wedding liturgy. Ask them with your choices in mind:

1) Will this song help all present to open themselves more fully to God? Will the song enhance the worship or distract from it?

2) What do the words say? (Get a copy of them or listen to them carefully, all the way through.) Do they express a Christian view of love or a shallow, Tin Pan Alley view? Are they theologically sound? Do they enhance your theme? Are they fitting for the celebration of the sacrament?

3) Does a particular selection fit the part of the ceremony where it occurs?

4) Does the type of music you have chosen draw people into real participation (active or passive) or lull them into being mere spectators?

5) Is the particular song within the capabilities of those singing and playing it?

6) Does the music have artistic merit or quality?

7) Has a particular number been overused at weddings?

Chapter Seven

Attending to Details

As a movie buff, I can recall being just a bit disillusioned when I discovered how movies were actually made: in disjointed scenes, shot out of sequence. Somehow, that took a little of the magic out of films for me.

So far, in "walking you through" the steps of wedding planning, I feel I've done something of the same—we've looked at some crucial elements (Scripture and music) and have touched upon isolated parts of the wedding liturgy out of sequence. Now it's time to restore a bit of order. As much as possible, I'd like to follow the wedding liturgy from start to finish, describing some of the options in each.

A note of caution: There is no way that I can cover *all* the options you have available. In describing the few that space allows, I trust I am not limiting your creativity. Nor do I want to rule out the richness that might flow from any of the many diverse cultural elements and customs which you might choose to stir into the final mix that will be your wedding liturgy. But since I can't possibly list them all, it's up to you, with your priest or deacon, to put flesh on the relatively bare-boned structure you'll find here.

That much said, let us begin by looking again at the major parts of the liturgy and the elements from which they are built.

The Entrance Rite

As your wedding liturgy begins, the Entrance Rite *creates a mood.* It changes a crowd of strangers who are coming to your wedding into an *assembly,* a more unified body with the goal of celebrating with you. The Entrance Rite sets the scene, and helps people get ready to pray.

The Prelude. One aspect of "scene setting" might be, as we hinted in the music chapter, a musical prelude, and—if desirable—an informal welcome and encouragement to sing and participate.

The prelude ought to begin when the first guests arrive, perhaps 20 minutes before the scheduled starting time. Here, some of the music you like which may not be as "liturgical" can be used. Instrumental or sung, the music ought to create a sense of quiet, reflection, prayer.

A brief song practice may be necessary if you are using unfamiliar music. Having the music leader encourage singing will further bond the assembly together. Be sure that there is some space between a practice and what comes next. Another quiet song or silence can mark the transition.

Greeting and Seating Guests. During this time, *greeting* takes place, a function most often given to your ushers. Encourage them to set a welcoming mood. Ask yourselves, too, why segregate bride and groom's families on opposite sides of the church? Does anyone really benefit from this old custom? Why not seat the immediate families on each side in the front, and then seat guests front to back so they can see and participate well?

Honoring Immediate Family. Most often, the settling of guests concludes with the seating of those persons you wish to single out for special honor. Grandparents, for example, may be escorted separately from the other guests. If they are not participating in an entrance procession, the mothers of the bride and groom are often given a special entrance.

Some couples have the mothers light two candles symbolizing the respective families; later the couple lights a third "unity" candle from the two. Both sets of parents could also fittingly perform this simple ritual. Music can accompany this moment.

Giving mothers special treatment in the entrance rite opens the question of the role of fathers. In the traditional wedding procession, the father of the bride "gives her away." Earlier, I spoke of the symbolism this holds: In previous centuries and cultures, brides were *property* to be "given away." Do you really want that symbol? If you do follow the custom, what role will you assign to the father of the groom?

The Wedding Procession. Two options seem more appropriate for contemporary weddings. One involves a "pre-entrance" of both sets of parents, accompanied by music. Together they can light candles symbolizing the families, if you are using the unity candle. They then take their seats and the main procession begins: Bridesmaids enter by way of the aisle and meet the groomsmen, who enter from another direction. The bride processes up the aisle and meets the groom at its head.

A second option, one that I prefer, involves an entrance procession of *couples*—after all, isn't that what marriage is about? The wedding party, men and women, enter as couples. Following the pairs of bridesmaids and groomsmen, the mother and father of the groom enter, flanking the groom. They process to the sanctuary and await the bride and her parents.

While this option breaks tradition, it fittingly symbolizes the unity we strive for in Christian marriage, and honors the role of parents in bringing their children to this moment.

Don't forget the presider! Tradition calls for the priest or deacon, with any servers, to wait at the altar for the couple to arrive. A more unified way, it seems to me, is to have a real procession involving everyone. Let the presider and other ministers (why not include the readers?) lead the procession into church with the couple following. This helps to symbolize that we are *all* part of the Church; not merely the priest or deacon waiting in the sanctuary.

Don't plan anything, by the way, without walking through your church long before the wedding day! With the priest or deacon, work out how a procession will look, where people will sit and what may be your best choice given the space you are using.

The Formal Welcome. Once you get in, it's time to welcome your guests. Most usually the presider does this, but it is also appropriate for the couple to share this welcome. The bride and groom can add a personal note and introduce the theme, if you wish. Such a shared greeting emphasizes your "couple-ness," that you are giving this sacrament to each other in the presence of family and friends, the Church.

Other Opening Rituals. After the welcome, when the wedding takes place at Mass, the penitential rite ("Lord, have mercy") is an opportunity to ask God to forgive our failure to love. (The "Glory to God," used on Sundays, is usually skipped at a wedding.) An opening prayer collects everyone's prayer sentiments and marks the end of the Entrance Rite.

The Liturgy of the Word

Chapter Five explored what goes into this second element of the wedding liturgy. Little remains to add, except for one consideration—choosing readers.

The Word of God deserves good readers, not family or friends chosen because you have to "find a place for them." This may be a role for parishioners who are lectors as a sign of your relationship to the local Church; those who helped prepare you for marriage might take on this role as well. Make sure that the readers have the text well in advance and have a chance to get comfortable with the place where they will read and the microphone.

The Liturgy of the Word concludes with the homily, given by the priest or deacon, or perhaps a clergy guest who is sharing the liturgy with you. You are free to suggest themes or special ideas you'd like the preacher to touch upon. Most will appreciate some personal thoughts from you.

The Rite of Marriage

This is a special, peak moment for you, as you "declare your consent before God and his Church" (*Rite of Marriage*, #25). Actually, it is the simplest part of the wedding liturgy—and that is as it should be. Your expression of consent—your marriage vows—ought to stand out clearly.

Arranging the Wedding Party. To preserve that simplicity, make sure that you "set up" this moment smoothly. The priest or deacon will call you forth, accompanied by the wedding party (among whom are your two principal witnesses, the best man and the maid or matron of honor).

In your walk-through in the empty church, plan out the best way to arrange the wedding party, making sure that they do not block the assembly's view. Getting them into place may take a moment or two. The musicians can provide simple background music if needed.

Work out the most comfortable way for the two of you to stand during this moment: facing the priest or deacon with your back to the people, facing each other or facing the assembly. Each of these positions for proclaiming your vows has its own effect—both on you and on the congregation. With your back to the congregation, you may be communicating a more private feeling about your ceremony. Facing each other emphasizes your relationship to each other. Facing the people really makes it clear that you are proclaiming something—and yet it may not be the easiest option. Choose what works best for you.

Presider's Introduction. The Rite of Marriage is introduced by the priest or deacon, using words that express something of the solemnity of the moment, the concept of sacrament and your intent to enter into marriage. This introduction includes three questions which ask you to state your intention: to enter into marriage freely, to remain faithful for life and to accept children as a fruit of the marriage, raising them in your faith. A simple, direct "yes" to these questions affirms your acceptance of the basic values which Catholics hold about the institution of marriage.

Declaration of Consent (Vows). Following your response, you are asked to join hands and declare your consent. Traditionally, the "I do" marked this moment, as couples responded to a question from the priest. More recent practice allows you to express your vows as a statement.

There are two forms—one, used less and less, contains the familiar and old-fashioned formula, "to have and to hold, from this day forward, for better, for worse...until death do us part" (*Rite of Marriage*, #25). Most couples opt for this shorter and simpler form:

> I, N., take you, N., to be my husband (wife). I promise to be true to you in good times and in bad, in sickness and in health. I will love you and honor you all the days of my life. (*Rite of Marriage*, #25)

Many couples choose to memorize this brief formula. The assisting priest or deacon holds a book nearby in case nervousness drives out the words. Other options include reading it from a book or card or repeating the words after the priest or deacon has said them. (Try to avoid this last choice, or at least ask the priest or deacon to *whisper* the words so you alone can hear them.)

In the 1960's and early 1970's, some couples chose to write their own vows. This practice has been discouraged in official liturgical practice, mainly for the reason mentioned above: simplicity. The statement of consent given here says in just a few well-chosen words what you are promising with your lives.

If you do feel a need to amplify this statement, you might want to write a fitting "couple prayer" and read it together at some point following the vows. My own recommendation is to let the simple, direct statement stand without adding more words. After all, *you* are the sign. Your presence in front of your family and friends speaks more loudly than a lot of extra words.

That gives rise to a more practical point: Be sure that when you speak your consent, you *can* be heard. A small microphone, discreetly held by the priest or deacon, may work. Or simply try to speak as clearly and distinctly as possible.

After the vows, the priest or deacon briefly affirms your consent. The ritual calls for an amen, but offers no obvious cue. I usually try to end the affirmation in such a way as to lead into an amen from the assembly. Such a response acts as a further yes to what you have just done. Another way to have the assembly assent is by means of a sung acclamation, although this is rarely done. The ritual text certainly seems to call for some kind of a vocal response at this point.

Exchange of Rings. Following your declaration of consent, you will exchange rings. Again, this is a simple ceremony in which the words are secondary to the action. There is a brief blessing prayer, and then you give the rings to each other with a simple statement which, again, can be either memorized, read or repeated. Be sure that someone has the rings within easy reach. I always discourage having them tied to a ring-bearer's pillow—especially after witnessing one disaster where a ring couldn't be unknotted.

Other Optional Ceremonies. The exchange of rings is sometimes followed by other ceremonies: the lighting of a unity candle, the signing of a marriage certificate or a short poem or meditation song. If you choose one of these, be sure that it is in harmony with the simple nature of the ritual you have just performed. Music can enhance these ceremonies and can also provide a transitional "distraction" as the wedding party returns to its seats.

Petitions. In a Mass, the General Intercessions (also known as the Prayer of the Faithful) concludes the Rite of Marriage. (In the liturgy outside of Mass, they also come at this point, but in a slightly different form which I will explain momentarily.)

Most of us are familiar with the petitions from Sunday Mass. Two basic principles apply to them: First, make sure they reflect a range of concerns from personal (prayers for the two of you, your family) to universal (the Church, the poor, other married couples). Second, keep them brief. Avoid wordiness and the cumbersome "For...that" formula ("For Howard and Claudia, that they may enjoy the blessing of married life").

Writing these petition-prayers is a personal, creative effort you ought to try. Avoid using ready-made formulas (that's why you won't find any "canned" versions in this book). The format is simple enough: You are making a request to God. State it simply and directly. For example, "God of life, you have brought George and Susan to this special day. Bless their love and their commitment to each other, we pray."

Invite a relative or friend to take a role by reading these prayer-requests on your behalf. Again, the basic principle: Choose a good reader, someone comfortable speaking before a group. Make sure he or she has the text well in advance and gets an opportunity to practice at the microphone.

If yours is an interfaith wedding and you are not celebrating in the context of Mass, the liturgy will conclude at this point with rituals which incorporate the petitions and other blessings and prayers. (See page 71 for details.)

66

The Liturgy of the Eucharist

When weddings are placed in the context of Mass, here begins the celebration of another sacrament—the gift of Jesus to us in the Eucharist. Your sacrament relates to it well, since you are making a gift of self to one another, as the Lord did to his disciples and to us at the Last Supper. It is appropriate, then, for this holy banquet to be a part of your wedding feast.

Presentation of the Gifts. The ritual "takes a breather" at this point, as the action makes a transition. The transitional moment is a time to "set the table." We used to call it the "Offertory," but that's a misnomer. What actually happens here is not an offering, but the preparation of the altar and of the things that will be used for the Eucharist.

Presenting the gifts of bread and wine is something you can ask family members or friends to do on your behalf. This usually is a "mini-procession" as the gifts are carried to the altar area. This is a good place to involve people whom you want to have special roles at your wedding.

Other items are sometimes brought forward as well (especially if you want to give roles to more than just two or three people), but those items should relate to the meal or table aspect of Eucharist. So, for example, the candles or even a tablecloth to be used on the altar may be carried in. Avoid other "symbolic" items, which tend to clutter up the simplicity of this special meal.

Homemade bread and wine may be appropriate at a wedding. There are guidelines for preparing these; check with the priest who is presiding at your Mass.

Quiet music is best for this time as the assembly relaxes just a bit from the intensity that has preceded. If you do have singing, don't use a song that will prolong the action.

Eucharistic Prayer. The high point of the Liturgy of the Eucharist is the proclamation of the Eucharistic Prayer. Here, the priest leads a solemn prayer that recalls what Jesus did at the Last Supper and begs God that the power of the Spirit will transform the gifts we have brought—and ourselves, so that we might be a sign of unity in the world.

You'll want to highlight this prayer in several ways. Consider asking the assembly to join you as a couple in *standing* throughout the prayer. (This will eliminate the clutter of kneelers and allow freer movement for the two of you.) Use singable acclamations, as we discussed in Chapter Six, to mark this moment: the "Holy, Holy," the Memorial Acclamation and the Great Amen. Your musician will be able to suggest well-known versions of these acclamations. (Reciting them is a less-than-desirable choice at such a festive occasion.)

The Lord's Prayer and Nuptial Blessing. Earlier we suggested *reciting* the Lord's Prayer rather than singing it, since this is a prayer most Christians are familiar with. Musical settings may actually distract here. Another gesture—asking the assembly to join hands—would highlight the unity we pray for.

Immediately following the Lord's Prayer is the Nuptial Blessing. There are several versions of this blessing available in the ritual. Choose the text which seems most appropriate (see page 112 in Appendix B).

(A caution: The nuptial blessing texts, of all the wedding liturgy texts, seem still to represent an older, culturally conditioned view of marriage which views the woman as somehow more in need of blessing. Work with your priest or deacon to understand and use these blessings in the most positive way possible.)

The priest will treat the prayer and the blessing as a unified element—perhaps by asking you to approach the altar (if you are not already close by) or by moving to the front of the altar, nearer the congregation.

Sign of Peace. After the blessing, we take time to express the "sign of peace" to one another and to our family and friends. Most couples want to extend this greeting at least to their parents and to the wedding party.

Flowers are sometimes given out to the mothers during this greeting. But take care not to prolong this time. Be aware of the seating arrangements and how far you must walk (especially in a wedding dress!) to give this greeting. A practical hint: Have the flowers waiting near the first pew, or have someone get the flowers into your hands so you don't have to retrieve them from somewhere else.

Again, your musicians can provide a song to enhance this moment, and such music can appropriately lead into another sung prayer, the "Lamb of God," which accompanies the breaking of the eucharistic bread and pouring of consecrated wine. During this latter gesture, those who are helping to distribute Communion can come to the altar area.

Reception of Communion. If both bride and groom are Catholic, the priest will offer the Eucharist to them first, usually under the form of both bread and wine. It is fitting to offer Communion under both forms to all communicants at the wedding as well; this fuller sign of eating *and* drinking more clearly reflects the meaning of Eucharist.

If you do offer the cup to your guests, you open up the possibility of yet another role for family members or friends who are trained as lay distributors or who, given local Church guidelines, may be commissioned for this occasion. Parishioners also may appropriately assist here. Consult your priest for more specific details.

Some priests invite the couple to assist in distributing Communion. I advise against this, since it seems to overburden the bride and groom, who have more than their share of things to be concerned with. Also, communicants may begin greeting the bride and groom

69

as they receive—an awkward situation I have witnessed on at least one occasion.

Music during Communion should be appropriate to the moment, fostering singing during the procession. It can be responsorial in nature, using a familiar refrain. A meditative song such as "Ave Maria" better fits in a post-Communion moment or as accompaniment to the devotion to Mary.

Optional Devotion to Mary. This long-standing custom usually involves having the bride and groom place flowers before a statue of Mary after Communion.

If you do choose this ritual, know *why* you wish to do it. If it represents devotion you have and a prayer you want to pray, that's a good reason! If it is a custom you are merely borrowing because you've seen it done, then you may be adding a ceremony merely for its own sake. It *is* optional, not a required part of the wedding liturgy.

If you choose this devotion, make sure it takes place in a space you can walk to conveniently. In one wedding I had, the bride and groom actually disappeared for five minutes, walking to a statue that was in some entrance area of the church! When you walk to the statue, stay there for a time of prayer that fits the song you have chosen to accompany the rite—don't just place the flowers and leave.

Concluding Prayer. The priest's Prayer After Communion ends the Liturgy of the Eucharist and moves us to the final part of the wedding.

The Dismissal Rite

Dismissing the assembly allows for a graceful transition to the next part of your wedding celebration, usually a meal or reception. By its nature, this rite is simple. It may include a presentation of the couple by the priest or deacon and appropriate "acclaim." (This presentation may also be done immediately following the vows and ring exchange earlier.)

Final Blessing. The final blessing offers a last moment of prayer. The assembly responds with "Amen" to the several petitions that make up the final blessing.

The Recessional. Traditionally, bride and groom lead the wedding party out of the church, accompanied by music—either a joyous instrumental or a rousing song to sing.

A word to the wise: Plan your exit well, deciding where a receiving line will be most appropriate. The time after the wedding liturgy can be full of many things: picture-taking in the church, a trip to the reception hall, greeting guests. You may want to "disappear" immediately after the ceremony, having alerted your guests that you will greet them at the reception. Customs and needs vary, so consider how best you can continue the celebration.

The Interfaith Setting: The Rite Without Mass

When a wedding is held outside of the context of Mass, the General Intercessions (petitions) are combined with the Nuptial Blessing. This is done in the following way: The presider (priest or deacon) introduces the petition-prayers; your reader presents the intercessions; the presider then offers the Nuptial Blessing.

After the Nuptial Blessing, the Lord's Prayer and a final blessing conclude the prayers, and the Dismissal Rite (see above) is underway. It is entirely appropriate to adapt the ritual to the demands of varying faith-traditions. So, for example, an ecumenically sensitive text of the Lord's Prayer might be used, as well as blessings and prayers from other traditions.

If a minister of another tradition is taking part, he or she will be able to suggest texts for use in this ritual. Special readings and hymns can create a truly ecumenical feeling. Ecumenical marriages, as noted earlier in this book, call for sensitivity and care. They can also be the opportunity for creative, instructive moments where the two of you can help others understand how the Spirit of God is creating a special unity in your lives.

Honoring Customs and Cultures

A planning guide such as this can only do so much. I cannot hope, as I stated earlier, to treat adequately all the rich variety of ethnic, racial and social customs that surround and enrich liturgical rites. Hymns in native languages, special gestures, rich colors in dress and decorations, alternative ways of arranging participants and prayers—all these should be explored in the context of who you are as a couple.

If you have not yet dipped into your own heritage, the occasion of your wedding may be a time of rediscovery. It also may be a way of honoring your family and sensitizing your guests to the rich possibilities that exist within our worship tradition. Now is the time to discover the old and create the new!

What Do You Want for Your Wedding?

Look back over the various options that have been presented. Begin discussing your wishes concerning some of the nonessential ceremonies: candlelighting, couple prayers, signing the marriage license, devotion to Mary. Ask yourselves first why you want to include any of these. Consider their impact on the whole celebration, and then choose accordingly.

From Appendix B, choose the prayers and blessings best suited to your theme.

Chapter Eight

People Make the Church— and Your Wedding

I n Chapter Three, I used the illustration of a parish church full of people as a way of explaining what Church was all about. I'd like to come back to that picture now, as a way of explaining what your wedding is all about. We began this planning process by discussing who you are as individuals and as a couple and how you relate to God and to the larger community.

Now imagine the church filled on your wedding day. Picture those who will be present, pew by pew. Imagine your parents, brothers and sisters, aunts and uncles, cousins. Mentally seat your friends and acquaintances. If you've already been making up an invitation list, this task of imagination will be easy.

It's this unique assembly—a gathering that has never before existed and will never exist again after your wedding day—that you are helping to create by entering into a marriage relationship. These are the people who love you, support you and challenge you. They will fulfill the important function of *witness* at your wedding. They need to see you standing up publicly to proclaim your love. You need to see them, present to affirm and encourage you and promising to stand by you through the years.

That mutual need ought to call forth a great sensitivity as you plan your wedding. Throughout this book, I have touched upon many *roles* which can be filled in the course of your wedding liturgy. Now you may want specifically to consider (if you have not already done so) how to match your "cast of characters," the special people you want to recognize and thank, to the many

73

roles that a wedding liturgy affords.

A Place for Parents

Parents are key people on a wedding day. They have a lot at stake in both of you. So their feelings are very important. You are bringing *two* sets of parents together, as well, so that calls for special attention to feelings.

Moms and Dads always have ideas about weddings—I don't need to tell you that, I'm sure. You have probably already gotten a lot of advice on the details of your wedding. Such advice represents important concerns and calls for understanding on your part.

At the same time, you need to make clear that your wedding is *your* celebration. By starting with sufficient time for good communication, you will avoid some last-minute hurt feelings. And you will preserve the important bonds that your parents symbolize and actually make present for you.

Along the way, I have suggested roles for parents to play in the liturgy itself: a place in the entrance procession, seats of honor, optional lighting of candles, presenting gifts. Choose the role that is most fitting after discussion with each other and with your parents.

Making Room for Your Family and Friends

The same principle applies to other family and friends. Seek input, but remember that *they* are not getting married; you are. And be aware of the creative ways we have suggested to allow others to participate in your ceremony beyond including them in the bridal party itself. Readers, ushers, gift-bearers, eucharistic ministers are the principal ones I have mentioned; your priest or deacon may suggest others.

Don't get locked into limited roles. Don't feel you need to include everyone in the wedding party itself, or that you inevitably have to exclude someone and therefore offend him or her. Rather, explore creative options. As mentioned earlier, there are easy ways to be inclusive. For example, the presentation of gifts might be a perfect time for a group of friends to take part. The Liturgy of the Word allows for two main readers and someone to help with the response. Later, more than one person can proclaim petitions. And the possibilities go on.

Let me add one more note of sensitivity: Be careful in your involvement of small children in your wedding. I have seen more than one ceremony interrupted because a cute child cast as a ring-bearer or flower girl panicked in the aisle. Remember that the church, a large crowd of strangers and the anxiety of the adults all affect a youngster—no matter how relaxed the rehearsal was.

Weigh how much distraction you are ready for versus the charming picture of a child in procession. There are other ways to involve your young relatives. Simply allowing them a grand entrance in their wedding outfits near the end of the prelude may fulfill your purpose.

Your Priest or Deacon as a Resource

The priest or deacon has, throughout this book, been my "fallback" as a resource. But more importantly, he is a sign of the Church. He acts as a focus for you, bringing to the moment of your sacramental sign the presence of the larger Church. In addition to the basic task of presiding at your wedding ceremony, he will also put you in touch with the options available for your ceremony, guide you through any legal requirements and be a sounding board for your wishes and questions.

This function is important because you are relating to a bigger reality—the Church as a community of people. This community has real needs, often expressed in such mundane things as getting the parking lot cleared for the next Mass. It's a complicated world, and we're in need of sensitive people to work together—even in planning a wedding. You as a couple can minister to your priest or deacon even as he ministers to you. By openness, listening and a sense of humor, the three of you can help to symbolize what your marriage in the Church really means.

Other Important People to Consider

You may be relying on other "experts" to assist in your wedding planning. Among these may be the *lay ministers from your parish wedding preparation team,* if you are lucky enough to have worked with a couple in examining the larger issues of marriage. Plan to include them in your wedding liturgy, if this seems appropriate.

Your *wedding party* is, no doubt, already playing a big role in your wedding planning. Remember that they are also crucial to the liturgical moment. The wedding rehearsal (see below) may be a time to remind them that they serve as symbols of how the Church supports your sacrament of marriage. The priest or deacon might appropriately describe this role as the rehearsal begins.

I have already touched upon the role of the *church musician* and the important resource this professional will be in your wedding. From my experience and that of musicians such as my brother, I know that a beautiful wedding (and, more importantly, a faith-experience) will come about in part from how you plan your music.

Other professionals may include the *photographer or videotaper* who helps to record your wedding. Most are professionals, who work discreetly and cooperatively with you and with your priest or deacon. But good communication helps.

Be sure you have adequately communicated just what you want in the way of a visual record. Be sure that all parish guidelines and the sensitivity of your presider are respected. (Flash photography or "prowling" video cameras can be very intrusive.) And remember, *you* are in charge of your wedding, its pace and its customs—not your photographer. He or she is at your service. Make sure you are clear on what that service includes.

Helping All to Participate

A final sensitive point in planning your wedding is *participation*. At Catholic weddings participation is often nonexistent. This isn't because strangers are present, I believe. Rather, it's just that we all have a lot on our minds. Because your guests will be thinking about the two of you, the reception to follow, who's walking in the door that they haven't seen in years and a million other things, it's a good idea to work out ways to help them participate once things start.

Having a worship aid—a wedding program—is an excellent way to encourage participation. This can take many forms; it can be very brief or quite detailed. Your priest or deacon can offer samples, perhaps; so can your church musician. (In fact, musicians often assist couples in assembling the printed program.) Your friends may have copies from their weddings. Remember to honor all copyright laws in reproducing words and music. Your church musician can help in that regard as well.

Welcoming your guests and setting a mood of relaxed celebration helps participation, too. Encourage your ushers to be gracious welcomers.

Bringing Your Wedding Party Together: The Rehearsal

All the important people who will make up your wedding will meet, usually for the first time, at the wedding rehearsal. This pre-wedding practice can be a time of awkwardness: People are nervous, perhaps uncomfortable in a church setting, unsure of what they have to do.

A good rehearsal depends on several things. First, make sure that the two of you are completely clear on what you want to do with the ceremony, especially where the members of the wedding party will walk, sit and stand. As I suggested earlier, do a walk-through with your priest or deacon in advance of the rehearsal so that

77

all of you understand the plans.

The priest or deacon will direct the rehearsal. He should make the group welcome and comfortable. A brief opening prayer helps to set the mood—what you are about to do *is* a prayer. Simple, clear instructions about what is going to happen, both during the rehearsal and in the wedding itself, will dispel a lot of the questions.

Be sensitive but firm when family and friends have suggestions on what to do. If you have made careful plans, stick to them. The priest or deacon can make it clear that, while you appreciate everyone's input and support, you will be following the plans you have made in order to help things run smoothly.

Remember, too, that over-rehearsing usually doesn't help. No wedding will be without some mistakes. Most often these can't be avoided, no matter how much preparation and practice you do.

That concern leads to a final point with regard to planning: I have seen weddings with elaborate plans, with so many details burdening the bride and groom that they really don't get to enjoy their wedding. You can avoid this if you rely on your family and friends as well as the Church professionals assisting you. It may help to delegate someone in the wedding party to track the details with you.

And it helps to remind yourselves to relax and know that your guests will be happy to share the day with you, no matter what happens. They will probably not notice if someone walks in the wrong direction or misses a cue or if some minor detail gets skipped. Once the ceremony begins, set aside your concern for all the details, take a deep breath, look into each other's eyes and let your wedding unfold.

A Final Resource

All that we've covered in this book is, as I've said several times, simply skimming the surface. There are many resources for you to turn to, but in the end, don't overlook two resources you may tend to forget in the course of planning: each other. You are the sacrament. You are the sign that is at the heart of your wedding. Look to that sign again and again—not only as you plan, but as you go on to the grander project that is the rest of your life together.

God be with you in *both* projects!

What Do You Want for Your Wedding?

Now it's time for *you* to make choices! Having brought together your own experience, learning, prayer and the advice of others, you have the opportunity to create a liturgical expression of your marriage commitment. In a way, this is a "sacramental" activity in itself: You are using the concrete signs of people, music, pageantry, poetry and much more to enflesh the deeper intangibles: love, trust, hope.

Getting specific means getting things down on paper. It might help first to line up the people you need to consider for roles in your wedding, along with the variety of roles available, as described in the text. You can match, add others and create new roles:

People
Parents
Brothers and sisters
Grandparents
Other relatives
Friends
Parish wedding preparation ministers
Priest or deacon
Other clergy
Other people

Roles
Best man and maid of honor
Ushers and bridesmaids
Readers (two main readings, response)

Reader for petitions
Communion distributors
Altar servers
Gift bearers
Photographer/videotaper
Church musicians
Other

Symbols. People need symbols, as mentioned
earlier. While you as a couple remain the principal
symbol at your wedding, there are many lesser
symbols and other items which you might find it
helpful to check off as you plan:

Flowers (for altar, bridal party, parents)
Programs
Special wedding candle
Aisle runner
Banners
Specially prepared bread and wine for Mass
Guest book for church vestibule/reception
Advance copies of readings/petitions for readers

The Final Plan. Now return to the planning guides
on pages 81 to 85. Use the notes you've made and the
sharing you've done throughout the process of working
through this book to complete the planning guides as
guides for your priest, deacon, musician and others who
will assist in your wedding. Good luck in planning!

Liturgy Planning Guide

(Note: You may wish to add a separate sheet that notes such additional items as booklet, banners, Communion meditation and so on.)

Groom: _____

Bride: _____

Priest/deacon: _____

Date and time of wedding: _____

Rehearsal: _____

Music provided by: _____

_____

_____

Theme of wedding: _____

Seating arrangement for wedding party: _____

_____

_____

Entrance Rite

Wedding Procession arrangement: _____

_____

_____

_____

Welcome prepared by: _____

Given by: _____

*Penitential Rite: Recited □ Sung □ I □ II □ III □

Introductory invocations for III _____

Opening Prayer: I □ II □ III □

*In a wedding celebrated outside of Mass, these elements are omitted.

81

Liturgy of the Word

Old Testament reading: _____

Reader: _____

Response: _____

Recited ☐ Sung ☐

Leader: _____

New Testament reading: _____

Reader: _____

Alleluia Verse: _____

Sung by (omit if not sung): _____

Gospel: _____

Read by: _____

Homily given by: _____

Rite of Marriage

Placement for exchange of vows: _____

_____

_____

Form of consent: I ☐ II ☐ Memorized ☐ Repeated after priest ☐
Read from card ☐

Blessing of Rings: I ☐ II ☐ III ☐

Additional ceremonies: _____

_____

_____

_____

General Intercessions prepared by: _____

Read by: _____

Liturgy of the Eucharist

*Gift-bearers: _____

_____

_____

*Prayer Over the Gifts: I ☐ II ☐ III ☐

*Preface to the Eucharistic Prayer: I ☐ II ☐ III ☐

*Holy, Holy: Sung ☐ Recited ☐

*Memorial Acclamation: I ☐ II ☐ III ☐ IV ☐ Other: _____

_____

*Great Amen: Sung ☐ Recited ☐

Our Father: Sung ☐ Recited ☐

Nuptial Blessing: I ☐ II ☐ III ☐

Greeting of Peace: _____

_____

*Communion Rite: Offer cup to bride and groom only ☐
To whole assembly ☐

Eucharistic ministers: _____

_____

_____

_____

Additional ceremonies: _____

_____

_____

Dismissal Rite

*Prayer After Communion: I ☐ II ☐ III ☐

Final blessing: I ☐ II ☐ III ☐

Music Planning Guide

(Note: Not all of the points in the liturgy given below need to be enhanced by instrumental music or singing; they are given merely for reference and discussion by planners.)

Prelude

_____

_____

_____

_____

Music practice before the liturgy: Yes ☐ No ☐

Entrance Rite

Processional: _____

Penitential Rite: _____

Liturgy of the Word

Response to Old Testament reading: _____

_____

Alleluia: _____

Rite of Marriage

Music following exchange of vows: _____

_____

Music to accompany additional ceremonies: _____

_____

_____

_____

_____

Liturgy of the Eucharist

Preparation of the Gifts: _____

_____

Holy, Holy: _____

Memorial Acclamation: _____

Great Amen: _____

Our Father: _____

Sign of Peace: _____

Lamb of God: _____

Communion songs: _____

_____

_____

_____

Meditation song after Communion: _____

_____

Additional ceremonies: _____

_____

_____

_____

Dismissal Rite

Recessional: _____

Postlude: _____

Appendix A

Scripture Readings

Old Testament Readings

1) Genesis 1:26-28, 31a

God said: "Let us make man in our image, after our likeness. Let them have dominion over the fish of the sea, the birds of the air, and the cattle, and over all the wild animals and all the creatures that crawl on the ground."

> God created man in his image;
>> in the divine image he created him;
>>> male and female he created them.

God blessed them, saying: "Be fertile and multiply; fill the earth and subdue it. Have dominion over the fish of the sea, the birds of the air, and all the living things that move on the earth...." God looked at everything he had made, and he found it very good.

2) Genesis 2:18-24

The LORD God said: "It is not good for the man to be alone. I will make a suitable partner for him." So the LORD God formed out of the ground various wild animals and various birds of the air, and he brought them to the man to see what he would call them; whatever the man called each of them would be its name. The man gave names to all the cattle, all the birds of the air, and all the wild animals; but none proved to be the suitable partner for the man.

So the LORD God cast a deep sleep on the man, and while he was asleep, he took out one of his ribs and closed up its place with flesh. The LORD God then built up into a woman the rib that he had taken from the man. When he brought her to the man, the man said:

"This one, at last, is bone of my bones
and flesh of my flesh;
This one shall be called 'woman,'
for out of 'her man' this one has been taken."

That is why a man leaves his father and mother and clings to his wife, and the two of them become one body.

3) Genesis 24:48-51, 58-67

[The servant of Abraham said to Laban:] "I bowed down in worship to the LORD, blessing the LORD, the God of my master Abraham, who had led me on the right road to obtain the daughter of my master's kinsman for his son. If, therefore, you have in mind to show true loyalty to my master, let me know; but if not, let me know that, too. I can then proceed accordingly."

Laban and his household said in reply: "This thing comes from the LORD; we can say nothing to you either for or against it. Here is Rebekah, ready for you; take her with you, that she may become the wife of your master's son, as the LORD has said...."

So they called Rebekah and asked her, "Do you wish to go with this man?" She answered, "I do." At this they allowed their sister Rebekah and her nurse to take leave, along with Abraham's servant and his men. Invoking a blessing on Rebekah, they said:

"Sister, may you grow
into thousands of myriads;
And may your descendants gain possession
of the gates of their enemies!"

Then Rebekah and her maids started out; they mounted their camels and followed the man. So the servant took Rebekah and went on his way.

Meanwhile Isaac had gone from Beer-lahai-roi and was living in the region of the Negeb. One day toward evening he went out...in the field, and as he looked around, he noticed that camels were approaching. Rebekah, too, was looking about, and when she saw him, she alighted from her camel and asked the servant, "Who is the man out there, walking through the fields toward us?" "That is my master," replied the servant. Then she covered herself with her veil.

The servant recounted to Isaac all the things he had done. Then Isaac took Rebekah into his tent; he married her, and thus she became his wife. In his love for her Isaac found solace after the death of his mother Sarah.

4) Tobit 7:9b-10, 11b-14

Tobiah said to Raphael, "Brother Azariah, ask Raguel to let me marry my kinswoman Sarah." Raguel overheard the words; so he said to the boy: "Eat and drink and be merry tonight, for no man is more entitled to marry my daughter Sarah than you, brother. Besides, not even I have the right to give her to anyone but you, because you are my closest relative. But I will explain the situation to you very frankly.... She is yours according to the decree of the Book of Moses. Your marriage to her has been decided in heaven! Take your kinswoman; from now on you are her love, and she is your beloved. She is yours today and ever after. And tonight, son, may the Lord of heaven prosper you both. May he grant you mercy and peace." Then Raguel called his daughter Sarah, and she came to him. He took her by the hand and gave her to Tobiah with the words: "Take her according to the law. According to the decree written in the Book of Moses she is your wife. Take her and bring her back safely to your father. And may the God of heaven grant both of you peace and prosperity." He then called her mother and told her to bring a scroll, so that he might draw up a marriage contract stating that he gave Sarah to Tobiah as his wife according to the decree of the Mosaic law. Her mother brought the scroll, and he drew up the contract, to which they affixed their seals.

Afterward they began to eat and drink.

5) Tobit 8:5-7

[On the wedding night Sarah] got up, and [she and Tobiah] started to pray and beg that deliverance might be theirs. He began with these words:

> "Blessed are you, O God of our fathers;
> praised be your name forever and ever.
> Let the heavens and all your creation
> praise you forever.

You made Adam and you gave him his wife Eve
    to be his help and support;
      and from these two the human race descended.
You said, 'It is not good for the man to be alone;
    let us make him a partner like himself.'
Now, Lord, you know that I take this wife of mine
    not because of lust,
      but for a noble purpose.
Call down your mercy on me and on her,
    and allow us to live together to a happy old age."

6) Song of Songs 2:8-10, 14, 16a; 8:6-7a

Hark! my lover—here he comes
    springing across the mountains,
    leaping across the hills.
My lover is like a gazelle
    or a young stag.
Here he stands behind our wall,
    gazing through the windows,
    peering through the lattices.
My lover speaks; he says to me,
    "Arise, my beloved, my beautiful one,
    and come!..."
"O my dove in the clefts of the rock,
    in the secret recesses of the cliff,
Let me see you,
    let me hear your voice,
For your voice is sweet,
    and you are lovely...."

My lover belongs to me and I to him....
      [He said to me:]
Set me as a seal on your heart,
    as a seal on your arm;
For stern as death is love,
    relentless as the nether world is devotion;
      its flames are a blazing fire.
Deep waters cannot quench love,
    nor floods sweep it away.

7) Sirach 26:1-4, 13-16

Happy the husband of a good wife,
　twice-lengthened are his days;
A worthy wife brings joy to her husband,
　peaceful and full is his life.
A good wife is a generous gift
　bestowed upon him who fears the Lord;
Be he rich or poor, his heart is content,
　and a smile is ever on his face....

A gracious wife delights her husband,
　her thoughtfulness puts flesh on his bones;
A gift from the Lord is her governed speech,
　and her firm virtue is of surpassing worth.
Choicest of blessings is a modest wife,
　priceless her chaste person.
Like the sun rising in the Lord's heavens,
　the beauty of a virtuous wife is the
　　radiance of her home.

8) Jeremiah 31:31-32a, 33-34a

The days are coming, says the Lord, when I will make a new covenant with the house of Israel and the house of Judah. It will not be like the covenant I made with their fathers the day I took them by the hand to lead them forth from the land of Egypt.... But this is the covenant which I will make with the house of Israel after those days, says the Lord. I will place my law within them, and write it upon their hearts; I will be their God, and they shall be my people. No longer will they have need to teach their friends and kinsmen how to know the Lord. All, from least to greatest, shall know me, says the Lord....

91

Responsorial Psalms

1) Psalm 33:12, 18, 20-22

Response: The earth is full of the goodness of the Lord.

Happy the nation whose God is the LORD,
    the people he has chosen for his own inheritance....
Response.

But see, the eyes of the LORD are upon
      those who fear him,
    upon those who hope for his kindness....
Response.

Our soul waits for the LORD,
    who is our help and our shield,
For in him our hearts rejoice;
    in his holy name we trust.
Response.

May your kindness, O LORD, be upon us
    who have put our hope in you. *Response*.

2) Psalm 34:2-9

Response: I will bless the Lord at all times. *Or*: Taste and see
the goodness of the Lord.

I will bless the LORD at all times;
    his praise shall be ever in my mouth.
Let my soul glory in the LORD;
    the lowly will hear me and be glad.
Response.

Glorify the LORD with me,
    let us together extol his name.
I sought the LORD, and he answered me
    and delivered me from all my fears.
Response.

Look to him that you may be radiant with joy,
    and your faces may not blush with shame.
When the afflicted man called out, the LORD heard,
    and from all his distress he saved him.

Response.

The angel of the Lord encamps
   around those who fear him, and delivers them.
Taste and see how good the Lord is;
   happy the man who takes refuge in him.

Response.

3) Psalm 103:1-2, 8, 13, 17-18a

Response: The Lord is kind and merciful. *Or:* The Lord's
kindness is everlasting to those who fear him.

Bless the Lord, O my soul;
   and all my being, bless his holy name.
Bless the Lord, O my soul,
   and forget not all his benefits....

Response.

Merciful and gracious is the Lord,
   slow to anger and abounding in kindness....
As a father has compassion on his children,
   so the Lord has compassion on those who fear him....

Response.

But the kindness of the Lord is from eternity
   to eternity toward those who fear him,
And his justice toward children's children
   among those who keep his covenant....

Response.

4) Psalm 112:1-9

Response: Happy are those who do what the Lord
commands. *Or:* Alleluia.

Happy the man who fears the Lord,
   who greatly delights in his commands.
His posterity shall be mighty upon the earth;
   the upright generation shall be blessed.

Response.

Wealth and riches shall be in his house;
   his generosity shall endure forever.

He dawns through the darkness, a light for the upright;
    he is gracious and merciful and just.

Response.

Well for the man who is gracious and lends,
    who conducts his affairs with justice;
He shall never be moved;
    the just man shall be in everlasting remembrance.

Response.

An evil report he shall not fear;
    his heart is firm, trusting in the LORD.
His heart is steadfast; he shall not fear
    till he looks down upon his foes.

Response.

Lavishly he gives to the poor;
    his generosity shall endure forever;
    his horn shall be exalted in glory.

Response.

5) Psalm 128:1-5

Response: Happy are those who fear the Lord. *Or*: See how
the Lord blesses those who fear him.

Happy are you who fear the LORD,
    who walk in his ways!
For you shall eat the fruit of your handiwork;
    happy shall you be, and favored.

Response.

Your wife shall be like a fruitful vine
    in the recesses of your home;
Your children like olive plants
    around your table.

Response.

Behold, thus is the man blessed
    who fears the LORD.
The LORD bless you from Zion:
    may you see the prosperity of Jerusalem
    all the days of your life....

Response.

6) Psalm 145:8-10, 15, 17-18

Response: The Lord is compassionate to all his creatures.

The LORD is gracious and merciful,
  slow to anger and of great kindness.
The LORD is good to all
  and compassionate toward all his works.

Response.

Let all your works give you thanks, O LORD,
  and let your faithful ones bless you....
The eyes of all look hopefully to you,
  and you give them their food in due season....

Response.

The LORD is just in all his ways
  and holy in all his works.
The LORD is near to all who call upon him,
  to all who call upon him in truth.

Response.

7) Psalm 148:1-4, 9-10, 11-14a

Response: Let all praise the name of the Lord. *Or*: Alleluia.

Praise the LORD from the heavens,
  praise him in the heights;
Praise him, all you his angels,
  praise him, all you his hosts.

Response.

Praise him, sun and moon;
  praise him, all you shining stars.
Praise him, you highest heavens,
  and you waters above the heavens....

Response.

You mountains and all you hills,
  you fruit trees and all you cedars;
You wild beasts and all tame animals,
  you creeping things and you winged fowl.

Response.

Let the kings of the earth and all peoples,
  the princes and all the judges of the earth,

95

Young men too, and maidens,
  old men and boys.
Response.

Praise the name of the LORD,
  for his name alone is exalted;
His majesty is above earth and heaven,
  and he has lifted up the horn of his people.
Response.

New Testament Readings

1) Romans 8:31b-35, 37-39

If God is for us, who can be against us? He who did not spare his own Son but handed him over for us all, how will he not also give us everything else along with him? Who will bring a charge against God's chosen ones? It is God who acquits us. Who will condemn? It is Christ [Jesus] who died, rather, was raised, who also is at the right hand of God, who indeed intercedes for us. What will separate us from the love of Christ? Will anguish, or distress, or persecution, or famine, or nakedness, or peril, or the sword? ...No, in all these things we conquer overwhelmingly through him who loved us. For I am convinced that neither death, nor life, nor angels, nor principalities, nor present things, nor future things, nor powers, nor height, nor depth, nor any other creature will be able to separate us from the love of God in Christ Jesus, our Lord.

2) Romans 12:1-2, 9-18 or
12:1-2, 9-13 (omit text in brackets { })

I urge you therefore, brothers, by the mercies of God, to offer your bodies as a living sacrifice, holy and pleasing to God, your spiritual worship. Do not conform yourself to this age but be transformed by the renewal of your mind, that you may discern what is the will of God, what is good and pleasing and perfect....

Let love be sincere; hate what is evil, hold on to what is good; love one another with mutual affection; anticipate one another in showing honor. Do not grow slack in zeal, be fervent in spirit, serve the Lord. Rejoice in hope, endure in affliction, persevere in prayer. {Contribute to the needs of the holy ones, exercise hospitality. Bless those who persecute [you], bless and do not curse them. Rejoice with those who rejoice, weep with those who weep. Have the same regard for one another; do not be haughty but associate with the lowly; do not be wise in your own estimation. Do not repay anyone evil for evil; be concerned for what is noble in the sight of all. If possible, on your part, live at peace with all.}

3) 1 Corinthians 6:13b-15a, 17-20

The body...is not for immorality, but for the Lord, and the Lord is for the body; God raised the Lord and will also raise us by his power. Do you not know that your bodies are members of Christ? ...But whoever is joined to the Lord becomes one spirit with him. Avoid immorality. Every other sin a person commits is outside the body, but the immoral person sins against his own body. Do you not know that your body is a temple of the holy Spirit within you, whom you have from God, and that you are not your own? For you have been purchased at a price. Therefore glorify God in your body.

4) 1 Corinthians 12:31—13:8a

Strive eagerly for the greatest spiritual gifts. But I shall show you a still more excellent way.

If I speak in human and angelic tongues but do not have love, I am a resounding gong or a clashing cymbal. And if I have the gift of prophecy and comprehend all mysteries and all knowledge; if I have all faith so as to move mountains, but do not have love, I am nothing. If I give away everything I own, and if I hand my body over so that I may boast but do not have love, I gain nothing.

Love is patient, love is kind. It is not jealous, [love] is not pompous, it is not inflated, it is not rude, it does not seek its own interests, it is not quick-tempered, it does not brood over injury, it does not rejoice over wrongdoing but rejoices with the truth. It bears all things, believes all things, hopes all things, endures all things.

Love never fails.

5) Ephesians 5:2b, 21-33 or
2b, 25-32 (omit text in brackets { })

[L]ive in love, as Christ loved us and handed himself over for us....

Be subordinate to one another out of reverence for Christ. Wives should be subordinate to their husbands as to the Lord. For the husband is head of his wife just as Christ is head of the church, he himself the savior of the body. As the church is subordinate to Christ, so wives should be subordinate to their husbands in everything. Husbands, love your wives, even as Christ loved the church and handed himself over for her, to sanctify her, cleansing her by the bath of water with the word, that he might present to himself the church in splendor, without spot or wrinkle or any such thing, that she might be holy and without blemish. So [also] husbands should love their wives as their own bodies. He who loves his wife loves himself. For no one hates his own flesh but rather nourishes and cherishes it, even as Christ does the church, because we are members of his body.

> "For this reason a man shall leave [his]
>   father and [his] mother
>   and be joined to his wife,
> and the two shall become one flesh."

This is a great mystery, but I speak in reference to Christ and the church. {In any case, each one of you should love his wife as himself, and the wife should respect her husband.}

6) Colossians 3:12-17

Put on then, as God's chosen ones, holy and beloved, heartfelt compassion, kindness, humility, gentleness, and patience, bearing with one another and forgiving one another, if one has a grievance against another; as the Lord has forgiven you, so must you also do. And over all these put on love, that is, the bond of perfection. And let the peace of Christ control your hearts, the peace into which you were also called in one body. And be thankful. Let the word of Christ dwell in you richly, as in all wisdom you teach and admonish one another, singing psalms, hymns, and spiritual songs with gratitude in your hearts to God. And whatever you do, in word or in deed, do everything in the name of the Lord Jesus, giving thanks to God the Father through him.

7) 1 Peter 3:1-9

[Y]ou wives should be subordinate to your husbands so that, even if some disobey the word, they may be won over without a word by their wives' conduct when they observe your reverent and chaste behavior. Your adornment should not be an external one: braiding the hair, wearing gold jewelry, or dressing in fine clothes, but rather the hidden character of the heart, expressed in the imperishable beauty of a gentle and calm disposition, which is precious in the sight of God. For this is also how the holy women who hoped in God once used to adorn themselves and were subordinate to their husbands; thus Sarah obeyed Abraham, calling him "lord." You are her children when you do what is good and fear no intimidation.

Likewise, you husbands should live with your wives in understanding, showing honor to the weaker female sex, since we are joint heirs of the gift of life, so that your prayers may not be hindered.

Finally, all of you, be of one mind, sympathetic, loving toward one another, compassionate, humble. Do not return evil for evil, or insult for insult; but, on the contrary, a blessing, because to this you were called, that you might inherit a blessing.

8) 1 John 3:18-24

Children, let us love not in word or speech but in deed and truth.

[Now] this is how we shall know that we belong to the truth and reassure our hearts before him in whatever our hearts condemn, for God is greater than our hearts and knows everything. Beloved, if [our] hearts do not condemn us, we have confidence in God and receive from him whatever we ask, because we keep his commandments and do what pleases him. And his commandment is this: we should believe in the name of his Son, Jesus Christ, and love one another just as he commanded us. Those who keep his commandments remain in him, and he in them, and the way we know that he remains in us is from the Spirit that he gave us.

9) 1 John 4:7-12

Beloved, let us love one another, because love is of God; everyone who loves is begotten by God and knows God. Whoever is without love does not know God, for God is love. In this way the love of God was revealed to us: God sent his only Son into the world so that we might have life through him. In this is love: not that we have loved God, but that he loved us and sent his Son as expiation for our sins. Beloved, if God so loved us, we also must love one another. No one has ever seen God. Yet, if we love one another, God remains in us, and his love is brought to perfection in us.

10) Revelation 19:1, 5-9a

After this I heard what sounded like the loud voice of a great multitude in heaven, saying:

"Alleluia!
Salvation, glory, and might belong to our God...."
A voice coming from the throne said:
"Praise our God, all you his servants,
[and] you who revere him, small and great."

Then I heard something like the sound of a great multitude or the sound of rushing water or mighty peals of thunder, as they said:

"Alleluia!
The Lord has established his reign,
[our] God, the almighty.
Let us rejoice and be glad
and give him glory.
For the wedding day of the Lamb has come,
his bride has made herself ready.
She was allowed to wear
a bright, clean linen garment."

(The linen represents the righteous deeds of the holy ones.)

Then the angel said to me: "Write this: Blessed are those who have been called to the wedding feast of the Lamb."

101

Alleluia Verses

1) God is love;
   let us love one another as he has loved us.
   (1 John 4:8b, 11b)

2) If we love one another,
   God will live in us in perfect love. (1 John 4:12)

3) He who lives in love, lives in God,
   and God in him. (1 John 4:16)

4) Everyone who loves is born of God and knows him.
   (1 John 4:7b)

Gospels

1) Matthew 5:1-12a

When [Jesus] saw the crowds, he went up the mountain, and after he had sat down, his disciples came to him. He began to teach them, saying:

> "Blessed are the poor in spirit,
> for theirs is the kingdom of heaven.
> Blessed are they who mourn,
> for they will be comforted.
> Blessed are the meek,
> for they will inherit the land.
> Blessed are they who hunger and thirst for righteousness,
> for they will be satisfied.
> Blessed are the merciful,
> for they will be shown mercy.
> Blessed are the clean of heart,
> for they will see God.
> Blessed are the peacemakers,
> for they will be called children of God.
> Blessed are they who are persecuted for the sake of righteousness,
> for theirs is the kingdom of heaven.

Blessed are you when they insult you and persecute you and utter every kind of evil against you [falsely] because of me. Rejoice and be glad, for your reward will be great in heaven."

2) Matthew 5:13-16

[Jesus said to his disciples:] "You are the salt of the earth. But if salt loses its taste, with what can it be seasoned? It is no longer good for anything but to be thrown out and trampled underfoot. You are the light of the world. A city set on a mountain cannot be hidden. Nor do they light a lamp and then put it under a bushel basket; it is set on a lampstand, where it gives light to all in the house. Just so, your light must shine before others, that they may see your good deeds and glorify your heavenly Father."

103

3) Matthew 7:21, 24-29 or
7:21, 24-25 (omit text in brackets { })

[Jesus said to his disciples:] "Not everyone who says to me, 'Lord, Lord,' will enter the kingdom of heaven, but only the one who does the will of my Father in heaven....

"Everyone who listens to these words of mine and acts on them will be like a wise man who built his house on rock. The rain fell, the floods came, and the winds blew and buffeted the house. But it did not collapse; it had been set solidly on rock. And everyone who listens to these words of mine but does not act on them will be like a fool who built his house on sand. The rain fell, the floods came, and the winds blew and buffeted the house. And it collapsed and was completely ruined."

{When Jesus finished these words, the crowds were astonished at his teaching, for he taught them as one having authority, and not as their scribes.}

4) Matthew 19:3-6

Some Pharisees approached [Jesus], and tested him, saying, "Is it lawful for a man to divorce his wife for any cause whatever?" He said in reply, "Have you not read that from the beginning the Creator 'made them male and female' and said, 'For this reason a man shall leave his father and mother and be joined to his wife, and the two shall become one flesh'? So they are no longer two, but one flesh. Therefore, what God has joined together, no human being must separate."

5) Matthew 22:35-40

[O]ne of [the Pharisees] [a scholar of the law] tested [Jesus] by asking, "Teacher, which commandment in the law is the greatest?" He said to him, "You shall love the Lord, your God, with all your heart, with all your soul, and with all your mind. This is the greatest and the first commandment. The second is like it: You shall love your neighbor as yourself. The whole law and the prophets depend on these two commandments."

6) Mark 10:6-9

[Jesus said:] "[F]rom the beginning of creation 'God made them male and female. For this reason a man shall leave his father and mother [and be joined to his wife], and the two shall become one flesh.' So they are no longer two but one flesh. Therefore what God has joined together, no human being must separate."

7) John 2:1-11

[T]here was a wedding in Cana in Galilee, and the mother of Jesus was there. Jesus and his disciples were also invited to the wedding. When the wine ran short, the mother of Jesus said to him, "They have no wine." [And] Jesus said to her, "Woman, how does your concern affect me? My hour has not yet come." His mother said to the servers, "Do whatever he tells you." Now there were six stone water jars there for Jewish ceremonial washings, each holding twenty to thirty gallons. Jesus told them, "Fill the jars with water." So they filled them to the brim. Then he told them, "Draw some out now and take it to the headwaiter." So they took it. And when the headwaiter tasted the water that had become wine, without knowing where it came from (although the servers who had drawn the water knew), the headwaiter called the bridegroom and said to him: "Everyone serves good wine first, and then when people have drunk freely, an inferior one; but you have kept the good wine until now." Jesus did this as the beginning of his signs in Cana in Galilee and so revealed his glory, and his disciples began to believe in him.

8) John 15:9-12

[Jesus said to his disciples:] "As the Father loves me, so I also love you. Remain in my love. If you keep my commandments, you will remain in my love, just as I have kept my Father's commandments, and remain in his love.

"I have told you this so that my joy might be in you and your joy might be complete. This is my commandment: love one another as I love you."

9) John 15:12-16

[Jesus said to his disciples:] "This is my commandment: love one another as I love you. No one has greater love than this, to lay down one's life for one's friends. You are my friends if you do what I command you. I no longer call you slaves, because a slave does not know what his master is doing. I have called you friends, because I have told you everything I have heard from my Father. It was not you who chose me, but I who chose you and appointed you to go and bear fruit that will remain, so that whatever you ask the Father in my name he may give you."

10) John 17:20-26 or 20-23 (omit text in brackets { })

[Jesus looked up to heaven and prayed:] "I pray not only for [my disciples], but also for those who will believe in me through their word, so that they may all be one, as you, Father, are in me and I in you, that they also may be in us, that the world may believe that you sent me. And I have given them the glory you gave me, so that they may be one, as we are one, I in them and you in me, that they may be brought to perfection as one, that the world may know that you sent me, and that you loved them even as you loved me. {Father, they are your gift to me. I wish that where I am they also may be with me, that they may see my glory that you gave me, because you loved me before the foundation of the world. Righteous Father, the world also does not know you, but I know you, and they know that you sent me. I made known to them your name and I will make it known, that the love with which you loved me may be in them and I in them."}

Appendix B
Prayers

Penitential Rite

1) I confess to almighty God,
    and to you, my brothers and sisters,
    that I have sinned through my own fault
    in my thoughts and in my words,
    in what I have done,
    and in what I have failed to do;
    and I ask blessed Mary, ever virgin,
    all the angels and saints,
    and you, my brothers and sisters,
    to pray for me to the Lord our God.

2) *Priest*: Lord, we have sinned against you:
    People: Lord, have mercy.

    Priest: Lord, show us your mercy and love.
    People: And grant us your salvation.

3) (Note: an introductory invocation is often used
    with this option.)
    Priest: Lord, have mercy.
    People: Lord, have mercy.

    Priest: Christ, have mercy.
    People: Christ, have mercy.

    Priest: Lord, have mercy.
    People: Lord, have mercy.

Opening Prayer

1) Father,
    you have made the bond of marriage
    a holy mystery,
    a symbol of Christ's love for his Church.

Hear our prayers for N. and N.
With faith in you and in each other
they pledge their love today.
May their lives always bear witness
to the reality of that love.

We ask this through our Lord Jesus Christ, your Son,
who lives and reigns with you and the Holy Spirit,
one God, for ever and ever.

2) Father,
hear our prayers for N. and N.,
who today are united in marriage before your altar.
Give them your blessing
and strengthen their love for each other.

We ask this through our Lord Jesus Christ, your Son,
who lives and reigns with you and the Holy Spirit,
one God, for ever and ever.

3) Almighty God,
hear our prayers for N. and N.,
who have come here today
to be united in the sacrament of marriage.
Increase their faith in you and in each other,
and through them bless your Church (with Christian
    children).

We ask this through our Lord Jesus Christ, your Son,
who lives and reigns with you and the Holy Spirit,
one God, for ever and ever.

4) Father,
when you created mankind
you willed that man and wife should be one.
Bind N. and N.
in the loving union of marriage
and make their love fruitful
so that they may be living witnesses
to your divine love in the world.

We ask this through our Lord Jesus Christ, your Son,
who lives and reigns with you and the Holy Spirit,
one God, for ever and ever.

Consent

1) I, N., take you, N., to be my wife/husband. I promise to be true to you in good times and in bad, in sickness and in health. I will love you and honor you all the days of my life.

2) I, N., take you, N., for my lawful wife/husband, to have and to hold, from this day forward, for better, for worse, for richer, for poorer, in sickness and in health, until death do us part.

Blessing of Rings

1) Lord, bless these rings which we bless in your name.
Grant that those who wear them
may always have a deep faith in each other.
May they do your will
and always live together
in peace, good will, and love.

We ask this through Christ our Lord.

2) Lord,
bless and consecrate N. and N.
in their love for each other.
May these rings be a symbol
of true faith in each other,
and always remind them of their love.

We ask this through Christ our Lord.

Prayer Over the Gifts

1) Lord,
accept our offering
for this newly-married couple, N. and N.
By your love and providence you have brought them together;
now bless them all the days of their married life.

We ask this through Christ our Lord.

2) Lord,
 accept the gifts we offer you
 on this happy day.
 In your fatherly love
 watch over and protect N. and N.,
 whom you have united in marriage.

 We ask this through Christ our Lord.

3) Lord,
 hear our prayers
 and accept the gifts we offer for N. and N.
 Today you have made them one in the sacrament of
  marriage.
 May the mystery of Christ's unselfish love,
 which we celebrate in this eucharist,
 increase their love for you and for each other.

 We ask this through Christ our Lord.

Preface

1) Father, all-powerful and ever-living God,
 we do well always and everywhere to give you thanks.
 By this sacrament your grace unites man and woman
 in an unbreakable bond of love and peace.

 You have designed the chaste love of husband and wife
 for the increase both of the human family
 and of your own family born in baptism.

 You are the loving Father of the world of nature;
 you are the loving Father of the new creation of grace.
 In Christian marriage you bring together the two orders
  of creation;
 nature's gift of children enriches the world
 and your grace enriches also your Church.

 Through Christ the choirs of angels
 and all the saints
 praise and worship your glory.
 May our voices blend with theirs
 as we join in their unending hymn:

2) Father, all-powerful and ever-living God,
 we do well always and everywhere to give you thanks

through Jesus Christ our Lord.

Through him you entered into a new covenant with your
people.
You restored man to grace in the saving mystery of
redemption.
You gave him a share in the divine life
through his union with Christ.
You made him an heir of Christ's eternal glory.

This outpouring of love in the new covenant of grace
is symbolized in the marriage covenant
that seals the love of husband and wife
and reflects your divine plan of love.

And so, with the angels and all the saints in heaven
we proclaim your glory
and join in their unending hymn of praise:

3) Father, all-powerful and ever-living God,
we do well always and everywhere to give you thanks.

You created man in love to share your divine life.
We see his high destiny in the love of husband and wife,
which bears the imprint of your own divine love.

Love is man's origin,
love is his constant calling,
love is his fulfillment in heaven.

The love of man and woman
is made holy in the sacrament of marriage,
and becomes the mirror of your everlasting love.

Through Christ the choirs of angels
and all the saints
praise and worship your glory.
May our voices blend with theirs
as we join in their unending hymn:

Memorial Acclamation

1) Christ has died,
   Christ is risen,
   Christ will come again.

2) Dying you destroyed our death,
   rising you restored our life.
   Lord Jesus, come in glory.

3) When we eat this bread and drink this cup,
   we proclaim your death, Lord Jesus,
   until you come in glory.

4) Lord, by your cross and resurrection,
   you have set us free.
   You are the Savior of the world.

Nuptial Blessing

(Note: From the alternate beginnings for Nuptial Blessings
1 and 2, choose the one which reflects your readings.)

1) Father, by your power you have made everything out of
   nothing.
   In the beginning you created the universe
   and made mankind in your own likeness.
   You gave man the constant help of woman
   so that man and woman should no longer be two,
   but one flesh,
   and you teach us that what you have united
   may never be divided.
   Or:
   Father, you have made the union of man and wife so holy
   a mystery
   that it symbolizes the marriage of Christ and his Church.
   Or:
   Father, by your plan man and woman are united,
   and married life has been established
   as the one blessing that was not forfeited by original sin
   or washed away in the flood.
   And:

112

Look with love upon this woman, your daughter,
now joined to her husband in marriage.
She asks your blessing.
Give her the grace of love and peace.
May she always follow the example of the holy women
whose praises are sung in the scriptures.

May her husband put his trust in her
and recognize that she is his equal
and the heir with him to the life of grace.
May he always honor her and love her
as Christ loves his bride, the Church.

Father, keep them always true to your commandments.
Keep them faithful in marriage
and let them be living examples of Christian life.

Give them the strength which comes from the gospel
so that they may be witnesses of Christ to others.
(Bless them with children
and help them to be good parents.
May they live to see their children's children.)
And, after a happy old age,
grant them fullness of life with the saints
in the kingdom of heaven.

We ask this through Christ our Lord.

2) Holy Father, you created mankind in your own image
   and made man and woman to be joined as husband and
       wife
   in union of body and heart
   and so fulfill their mission in this world.

Or:

Father, to reveal the plan of your love,
you made the union of husband and wife
an image of the covenant between you and your people.
In the fulfillment of this sacrament,
the marriage of Christian man and woman
is a sign of marriage between Christ and the Church.

And:

Father, stretch out your hand, and bless N. and N.

Lord, grant that as they begin to live this sacrament
they may share with each other the gifts of your love

and become one in heart and mind
as witnesses to your presence in their marriage.
Help them to create a home together
(and give them children to be formed by the gospel
and to have a place in your family).

Give your blessings to N., your daughter,
so that she may be a good wife (and mother),
caring for the home,
faithful in love for her husband,
generous and kind.
Give your blessings to N., your son,
so that he may be a faithful husband
(and a good father).
Father, grant that as they come together to your table
  on earth,
so that they may one day have the joy of sharing your
  feast in heaven.

We ask this through Christ our Lord.

3) Holy Father, creator of the universe,
maker of man and woman in your own likeness,
source of blessing for married life,
we humbly pray to you for this woman
who today is united with her husband in this sacrament
  of marriage.

May your fullest blessing come upon her and her
  husband
so that they may together rejoice in your gift of married
  love
(and enrich your Church with their children).

Lord, may they both praise you when they are happy
and turn to you in their sorrows.
May they be glad that you help them in their work
and know that you are with them in their need.
May they pray to you in the community of the Church,
and be your witnesses in the world.
May they reach old age in the company of their friends,
and come at last to the kingdom of heaven.

We ask this through Christ our Lord.

(R) Amen.

114

Prayer After Communion

1) Lord,
   in your love
   you have given us this eucharist
   to unite us with one another and with you.
   As you have made N. and N.
   one in this sacrament of marriage
   (and in the sharing of the one bread and the one cup),
   so now make them one in love for each other.

   We ask this through Christ our Lord.

2) Lord,
   we who have shared the food of your table
   pray for our friends N. and N.,
   whom you have joined in marriage.
   Keep them close to you always.
   May their love for each other
   proclaim to all the world
   their faith in you.

   We ask this through Christ our Lord.

3) Almighty God,
   may the sacrifice we have offered
   and the eucharist we have shared
   strengthen the love of N. and N.,
   and give us all your fatherly aid.

   We ask this through Christ our Lord.

Final Blessing

1) May God the eternal Father keep you in love with each
       other,
   so that the peace of Christ may stay with you
   and be always in your home.

   (R) Amen.

   May (your children bless you,)
   your friends console you
   and all men live in peace with you.

   (R) Amen.

May you always bear witness to the love of God in this
    world
so that the afflicted and the needy
will find in you generous friends,
and welcome you into the joys of heaven.

(R) Amen.

And may almighty God bless you all,
the Father, the Son, and the Holy Spirit.

(R) Amen.

2) May God, the almighty Father,
give you his joy
and bless you (in your children).

(R) Amen.

May the only Son of God have mercy on you
and help you in good times and bad.

(R) Amen.

May the Holy Spirit of God
always fill your hearts with his love.

(R) Amen.

And may almighty God bless you all,
the Father, the Son, and the Holy Spirit.

(R) Amen.

3) May the Lord Jesus, who was a guest at the wedding in
    Cana,
bless you and your families and friends.

(R) Amen.

May Jesus, who loved his Church to the end,
always fill your hearts with his love.

(R) Amen.

May he grant that, as you believe in his resurrection,
so you may wait for him in joy and hope.

(R) Amen.

And may almighty God bless you all,
the Father, the Son, and the Holy Spirit.

(R) Amen.